The eighth edition of
the Best of European
Design and Advertising
from the Art Directors
Club of Europe 1999

AD&E 8

willkommen willkommen

välkommen

bienvenido

WE

benvenuto

fáilte

welkom

willkommen

begroeten

willkommen

The Art Directors Club of Europe (ADCE) was founded in June 1990 as a not-for-profit organisation to foster and reward creative excellence in European Design and Advertising. ADCE is managed and owned by 10 representative national bodies across Europe. Each of these organisations has a membership of leading professional creatives and each one also runs its country's premier awards scheme.

On Saturday 5 June 'The Best of European Design and Advertising Awards 1999', hosted by ADCE, was held at the Design Council in London. Four senior creatives per country travelled to London to judge this body of work making a total jury of up to 44 leading art directors, copywriters, designers, photographers and commercials directors. They selected Gold awards in each category and an overall Grand Prix.

In total there were 300 European entries in 21 categories. All the entries have already won a Silver or Gold Award in their countries national competition, so the ADCE Gold and Grand Prix winners are awarded from the "best of the best". All of these pieces are featured in the Annual providing a unique European archive.

The book is distributed to all the 9,500 members of all the individual national clubs and is also sold in bookshops around the world.

PRESIDENT'S STATEMENT

Fernando Gutiérrez

Tough. Authoritative. Inspiring. Essential ingredients for a top international award scheme and the Art Directors Club of Europe has these in abundance.

Tough, because there are well over 50,000 pieces of work entered to the ten national schemes across Europe; only 300 make it into this book by winning their country's top honours; only 10 of the 300 won an Art Directors Club of Europe Gold; there is only one Grand Prix winner – the stunning cinema commercial, 'Litany', by Lowe Howard-Spink for the UK's Independent newspaper. One out of fifty thousand. Any bookie will agree – that's tough!

Authoritative, because these Awards are owned and run, not-for-profit, by the major national associations representing creative professionals in their respective countries. The joint memberships total over 8,000 leading designers, art directors, copywriters, creative directors, film makers, illustrators and photographers. Quite a mandate.

Inspiring, well, you decide. Certainly the team of international judges who gathered in London last June to select the winners thought so....

A special thanks to those who make the Arts Directors Club of Europe such a success!

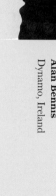

Alan Bennis
Dynamo, Ireland

Theophil Butz
Bosch & Butz, Switzerland

Dominique Van Doormaal
Saatchi & Saatchi, Belgium

Mark Farrow
Farrow Design, UK

Fernando Gutiérrez *President*
Spain

Niels Meulman
Caulfield & Tensing, Netherlands

Giorgio Nataie
Ammirati Puris Lintas, Italy

Mike Ries
Jung von Matt am Main, Germany

Anders Wallskog
Brindfors Design, Sweden

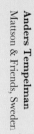

Andre Aimaq
Aimaq Rapp Stolle, Germany

Tibor Bárci
Bárci & Partner, Austria

Monica Kruisman
JWT, Belgium

Danielle Lanz
Guy & Partner, Switzerland

Adrian Fitz-Simon
Irish International, Ireland

David Ruiz
David Ruiz & Marina Company, Spain

Matt Ryan
Saatchi & Saatchi, UK

Othmar Severin *Chairman*
Germany

Anders Tempelman
Mattson & Friends, Sweden

Béla Stamenkovits
TBWA/Campaign Company, Netherlands

Rogier van der Ploeg
Czar Films, Netherlands

John Kane
Javelin Young & Rubicam, Ireland

Johannes Krammer
Demner, Merlicek & Bergmann, Austria

Steven Grounds
The Hollies, UK

Lars Hansson
Hall & Cederquist/Y&R, Sweden

Jamie Ambler
McCann Erickson, Belgium

Johannes Newrkla Chairman
Demner, Merlicek & Bergmann, Austria

Aldo Cernuto
Pirella Gottsche Lowe, Italy

Jan Ritter
Springer & Jacoby, Germany

Jose Gamo
Tiempo/BBDO, Spain

Barbara Strahm
Wirz Werbeberatung AG, Switzerland

Cordula Alessandri
Austria

Wolfgang Behnken
Gruner Jahr Stern Magazine, Germany

Marco Calant *Chairman*
Publicis, Belgium

Ciro Falavigna
Italy

Michael Kenny
Freelance, Ireland

Jacques Koeweiden
Koeweiden Postma, Netherlands

Michel De Lauw
DDB, Belgium

Hans Tanner
WEber Hodel Schmid, Switzerland

Brian Webb
Tricket & Webb, UK

Austria
Creativ Club Austria
Kochgasse 34/16
Vienna 1080
tel: + 43 1 408 53 51
e-mail: cca-buero@eunet.at

Belgium
Creative Club Of Belgium
4 Rue Jean d'Ardenne
1050 B Brussels
tel: + 322 511 4969

Germany
Art Directors Club für Deutschland
Melemstrasse 22
60322 Frankfurt am Main
tel: +49 69 596 4009
e-mail: adc@adc.de

Ireland
Institute Of Creative Advertising & Design
31 Heytesbury Lane
Dublin 4
tel: + 353 1 660 1590

Italy
Art Directors Club Italiano (ADCI)
Via Sant'Orsola 1
20123 Milano
tel: +39 02 804 633
e-mail: adci@essai.it

The Netherlands
WG Plein 504
Amsterdam 1054 SJ
tel: +31 20 685 0861
e-mail: adcn@wxs.nl

Spain
ADG.FAD
Carrer Brusi 45
Barcelona 08006
tel: + 34 93 200 24 29

Sweden
Sveriges Reklamförbund
(The Advertising Association of Sweden)
Norrlandsgatan 24
Box 1420
111 84 Stockholm
Tel: +46 8 679 08 00
e-mail: info@reklam.se

Switzerland
Art Directors Club Schweiz
Oberdorfstr. 15
Zürich 8001
Tel: +41 1 262 00 33
e-mail: adc@bluewin.ch

UK
British Design & Art Direction
9 Graphite Square
Vauxhall Walk
London SE11 5EE
Tel: +44 207 840 1133
e-mail: info@dandad.co.uk

Board of Directors

President
Fernando Gutiérrez Spain

Treasurer
Johannes Newrkla Austria

Controller
David Kester UK

Johannes Newrkla Austria
Marco Calant Belgium
Othmar Severin Germany
Mark Nutley Ireland
Franco Moretti Italy
Luigi Montaini Anelli Italy
Krijn Van Noordwijk The Netherlands
Fernando Gutiérrez Spain
Mårten Brink Sweden
Martin Spillmann Switzerland

Administration

Art Directors Club of Europe
9 Graphite Square
Vauxhall Walk
London SE11 5EE
Tel: + 44 207 840 1133
Fax: + 44 207 840 0840
Email: tracy@dandad.co.uk

Co-ordinator
Tracy Breeze

CONTENTS

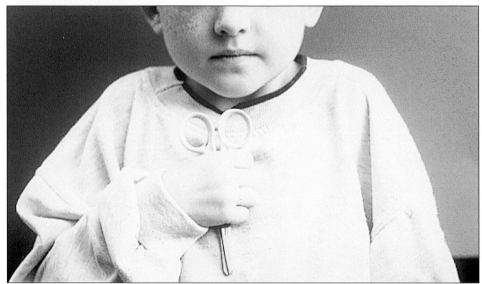

Grand Prix Award **TV & Cinema Advertising** **Cinema Commercial**
National Award Silver **Title** Litany **Agency** Lowe Howard-Spink **Client** The Independent Newspaper **Creative Director** Paul Weinberger **Art Director** Charles Inge
Copywriter Charles Inge **Agency Producer** Charles Crisp **Director** Rob Sanders **Production Company** HLA **Editor** Tim Fulford **Lighting Camera** Bob Pendar - Hughes
Music Composers Joe Campbell, Paul Hart **Producer** Helen Langridge

Life's pleasures are often frowned upon: this list of don'ts ("Don't fry your food, do drugs, breathe...") alludes to the free spirit of the paper's readers.

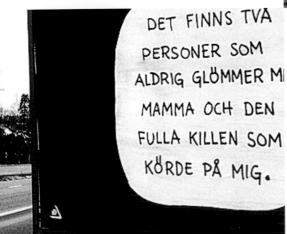

DET FINNS TVA
PERSONER SOM
ALDRIG GLÖMMER MI
MAMMA OCH DEN
FULLA KILLEN SOM
KÖRDE PÅ MIG.

BEST OF THE BEST

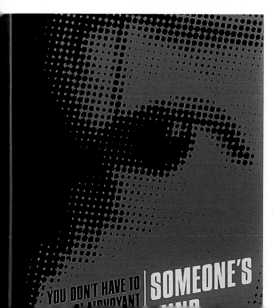

austria

AU
ST
R
A

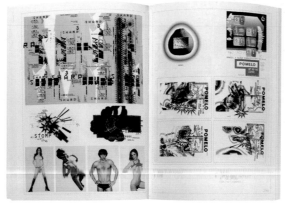
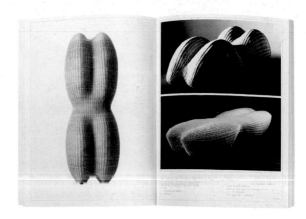

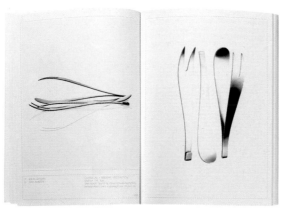

1   **Nomination   Editorial**
National Award Silver **Title** Design Now. Austria **Design Studio** Büro X Design GmbH **Client** Eichinger oder Knechtl on behalf of the Federal Chancellary Arts Department
Creative Directors Andreas Miedaner, Günter Eder **Art Director** Günter Eder **Copywriters** Reiner Zettl, Eichinger oder Knechtl

Catalogue for Design Now. Austria - An Exhibition of Contemporary Austrian Design.

2   **Nomination   Editorial**
National Award Gold **Title** Wallpaper **Agency** Section.d haupt-stummer.jasensky.winkler.design **Client** Time Inc **Art Director** Herbert Winkler **Designer** Richard Spencer - Powell

17 Austria

3 **Nomination   Illustration & Photography   Illustration**
National Award Gold **Title** Homosexuality **Agency** Lowe GGK **Client** HOSI (Homosexuality initiative) Linz **Creative Director** Walther Salvenmoser **Art Director** Daniel Gantner
Copywriter Walther Salvenmoser **Illustrator** René Habermacher

4 **Nomination   Illustration & Photography   Illustration**
National Award Silver **Title** Fusion Cooking/Stephen King **Agency** Section.d haupt.stummer.jasensky.winkler.design **Client** De Agostini Rizzoli Periodici/ Milano
Creative Director Herbert Winkler **Art Director** Herbert Winkler **Illustrator** Anja Kroenke

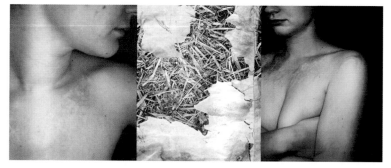

5 **Nomination   Illustration & Photography   Photography**
National Award Silver **Title** Wittmania **Agency** Czerny, Celand, Plakolm Werbeges. m.b.H **Client** Wittmann Möbelwerksättenges m.b.H **Creative Directors** Gerhard Plakolm, Elfie Semotan
Art Director Gerhard Plakolm **Photographer** Elfie Semotan

6 **Nomination   Illustration & Photography   Photography**
National Award Gold **Title** Liebe Wunden (Beloved Wounds) **Entrant** Markus Rössle **Client** Markus Rössle **Photographer** Markus Rössle

Tex Rubinowitz zwischen Strich und Punkt.

Aus dem Wiener Wasserhähnen läuft seit 125 Jahren wertvolles Hochquellwasser. Auch Herr Tex Rubinowitz, Cartoonist und Geschichtenschreiber, erfreut sich an diesem kostbaren Naß.

Otto Wanz zwischen Telefonbuch und Expander.

Aus dem Wiener Wasserhähnen läuft seit 125 Jahren wertvolles Hochquellwasser. Auch Herr Otto Wanz, Catcher, hat auf der ganzen Welt noch nichts Vergleichbares getrunken.

Leopold Hawelka zwischen kleinen Braunen und großen Gästen.

Aus dem Wiener Wasserhähnen läuft seit 125 Jahren wertvolles Hochquellwasser. Auch Herr Leopold Hawelka, Kaffeesieder, trinkt es gerne.

Josefine Hawelka zwischen Buchteln und Sperrstunde.

Aus dem Wiener Wasserhähnen läuft seit 125 Jahren wertvolles Hochquellwasser. Auch Frau Josefine Hawelka, Kaffeesiederin, will es keinesfalls missen.

9

DER UNTERSCHIED IST EIN UNFALL.
AKTION MENSCH
ODER: WIE SIE LERNEN, IHR ZWEITES ICH ZU LIEBEN.

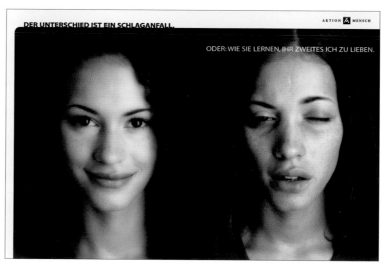

DER UNTERSCHIED IST EIN SCHLAGANFALL.
AKTION MENSCH
ODER: WIE SIE LERNEN, IHR ZWEITES ICH ZU LIEBEN.

10

9 **Print Advertising   Magazine Advertising**
National Award Silver **Title** The Viennese enjoy mountain spring water **Agency** Strobelgasse 2 Werbeagentur GmbH **Client** Wiener Wasserwerke **Creative Director** Björn Forgber
Art Director Jeff Stenzenberger **Copywriters** Björn Forgber, Wolfgang Hummelberger **Photographer** Stefan Liewehr

Headline : Tex Rubinowitz in between dots and dashes. Copy: Precious mountain water has been running out of Viennese taps for the past 125 years. Tex Rubinowitz, cartoonist and author, also enjoys this valuable water. Headline: Otto Wanz in between telephone books and expander. Copy: Precious mountain spring water has been running out of Viennese taps for the past 125 years. Otto Wanz, Catcher, also has not drunk anything comparable anywhere on the world. Headline: Leolpold Hawelka in between small coffees and famous guests. Copy: Precious mountain spring water has been running out of Viennese taps for the past 125 years. Leopold Hawelka, Coffeehouse proprietor, also likes to drink it. Headline: Josefine Hawelka between sweet pudding and closing time. Copy: Precious mountain spring water has been running out of Viennese taps for the past 125 years. J. Hawelka, Coffeehouse proprietor, also would like to do without it.

10 **Print Advertising   Magazine Advertising**
National Award Gold **Title** The difference is an accident. Or: how to love your second self. **Agency** Lowe GGK **Client** Eltern in Sorge (Concerned parents)
Creative Directors Walther Salvenmoser, Christian Satek **Art Director** Elke Bocksrucker **Copywriter** Walther Salvenmoser **Photographer** Dieter Brasch

21 Austria

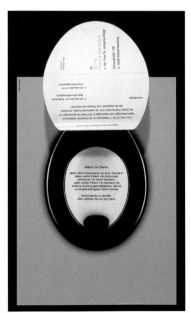

Nach den „100 Wörtern des Jahrhunderts": Hier sind

DIE 10 WÖRTER DES JAHRTAUSENDS.

Wie Sie wahrscheinlich den Medien entnommen haben, präsentierte dieser Tage eine hochkarätige Fachjury die sorgfältig ausgewählten „100 Wörter des Jahrhunderts". Jene Begriffe also, die in ihrer Substanz am ehesten dazu geeignet seien, unser ausgehendes Centennium hinreichend zu charakterisieren. Düstere Worte wie „Terrorismus", „Panzer" oder „Blockwart" waren dabei, aber auch hoffen machende wie „Beat", „Kugelschreiber", „Kreditkarte" oder „Camping". Jetzt glauben wir vom Andreas Putz Textbüro jedoch, daß der Blick einzig auf die letzten 100 Jahre nicht weit genug reicht. Schließlich stehen wir nicht nur am Ende eines Jahrhunderts, sondern, viel bedeutender noch, am Ende eines ganzen Jahrtausends. Und so – Sie werden sich wegen der Überschrift möglicherweise schon sowas gedacht haben – möchten wir Ihnen also aus aktuellem Anlaß die zehn Begriffe vorstellen, deren Bedeutung eine hochkarätige Fachjury als am vergleichsweise wichtigsten im langen Zeitraum der letzten 1000 Jahre erkannt hat. Es sind dies:

1: Seybarer
2: Pestilenz
3: Maschelle
5: Schwerkraft
6: Skorbut
7: Myrenarithum
8: Weihnachtsgruß
9: Sextant
10: Bünduer

Dieser oder jener wird nun vielleicht sagen, bei dem einen oder anderen Wort könne es sich doch wohl nur um das Ergebnis einer krassen Fehlentscheidung handeln. Ein Begriff wie „Weihnachtsgruß" beispielsweise sei doch wohl völlig unbedeutend für die Entwicklung der Menschheit. Vielleicht wird dieser oder jener anschließend seinen Winterrotz aufziehen und empört ausspucken. Festen Blickes antworten wir: Wie kleinmütig Sie doch sind! Natürlich ist ein Wort wie „Weihnachtsgruß" von Bedeutung! Von immenser sogar! Denn gäbe es dieses Wort nicht, was sollten wir Ihnen denn jetzt übermitteln? Ein Myrenarithum vielleicht?

11 **Print Advertising   Trade Advertising**
National Award Gold **Title** Bitte Öffnen (Toilet Lid) **Agency** Barci & Partner **Client** Solvay Pharma GesmbH **Creative Director** Dr. Gerald Shorter **Art Director** Christine Kriegler **Copywriter** Dr. Gerald Shorter **Photographer** Wolfgang Werzowa **Illustrator** Christine Kriegler

Please open. Irritated intestines should be treated. Act by using the card.

12 **Print Advertising   Trade Advertising**
National Award Silver **Title** The 10 Words of the Millennium **Agency** Andreas Putz Textbuero **Client** Andreas Putz **Creative Directors** Andreas Putz, Günter Eder **Copywriter** Günter Eder **Designer** Andreas Putz

The 10 words of the Millennium.

22 Austria

13 **TV & Cinema Advertising   Television Commercial**
National Award Silver **Title** Crest "In front of the mirror" **Production Company** Mican Werbefilmproduktion GmbH **Client** Doetsch Grether AG **Creative Director** Robert Stalder
Art Director Daniel Kaeser **Film Director** Guntmar Lasnig **Director of Photography** Gero Lasnig

Teenager, preparing herself for a date.

14 **TV & Cinema Advertising   Television Commercial**
National Award Gold **Title** In 7ieben Tagen um die Welt "Diashow" 1998 **Agency** Heye & Partner, Wien **Client** McDonald's Austria **Creative Directors** Alexander Bartel, Martin Kiessling
Art Director Frank Widmann **Copywriter** Martin Kiessling **Agency Producer** Janet Fox **Film Director** Neil Harris **Production Company** Arden Sutherland Dodd

Headline: Around the world in seven days.

15 **TV & Cinema Advertising   Cinema Commercial**
   National Award Silver **Title** Hooch "London Underground" **Agency** Goldfish **Client** Brau Union AG **Creative Directors** Franz Weissenböck, Wien Nord **Film Director** Stefan Ruzowitzky
   Production Company PPM Filmproductions

   England's revenge on boredom.

16 **Posters   Poster Advertising**
   National Award Gold **Title** 1) Während der Fahrt nicht mit dem Fahrer sprechen 2) Nachtruhe ab 19.00 Uhr 3) Für Garderobe wird keine Haftung übernommen 4. Bitte Festhalten
   Agency ORF - Grafik **Client** Radio FM4 - Austrian Broadcasting **Creative Director** Michael Hajek **Art Director** Sabine Brauner **Copywriter** Sabine Brauner **Photographer** Slava Filipov

   1) Please do not distract the driver 2) Night time peace from 7pm 3) We accept no responsibility for clothing. 4. Please hold tight.

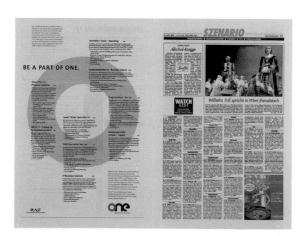

17 Posters   Poster Advertising
National Award Silver **Title** Test-Aufruf **Agency** Weber, Hodel, Schmid **Client** Connect Austria **Creative Director** Beat Egger **Art Director** Jürg Aemmer **Copywriters** Beat Egger, Andreas Putz **Designers** Sasha Huber, Alex Trüb

Test-Call: Test the mobile communication network of tommorow. Thank you Tirol, thank you Vorarlberg. Your "Connect Austria". Test telephone: 0699 170 800.

18 Promotion
National Award Gold **Title** The Blue Standard **Agency** DMC Design for Media and Communication GmbH & Co KG **Client** Connect Austria GmbH **Creative Directors** Markus Huber, Stefan Pott , Hubert Schillhuber **Art Directors** Rudi Zündel, Markus Huber **Designer** Sylvia Kostenzer

"The Standard" (newspaper), normally pink, was printed on blue paper for the launch of ONE.

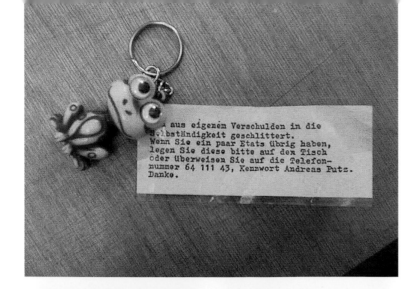

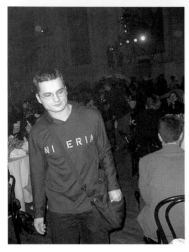

19

20

Original-Schneeflocke aus Enverslund,
dem Heimatort von Santa Claus.

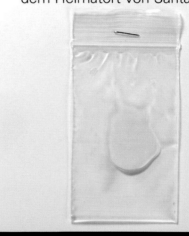

Als am 23. September 1998 der erste Schnee in Enverslund/Nordnorwegen fiel, herrschte mit einem Schlag reges Treiben in den ortsansässigen Kindergärten und Schulklassen. Denn dort wurden in liebevoller Kleinarbeit flugs die ersten Zeugnisse des nahenden Winters verpackt, um Ihnen als kleiner Weihnachtsgruß gefällig zu sein. Die beiliegende Schneeflocke aus Enverslund (das ja, wie oben erwähnt, der Heimatort von Santa Claus ist) widmen Ihnen alle MitarbeiterInnen von dietheater Wien: Minka Benovic-Fellner, Rudolf Burscher, Helmut Drucker, Bärtl Grammel, Karl Grünböck, Helga Hofinger, Saskia Hölbling, Harald Jokesch, Rudolf Katzer, Andrea Korcsoc, Ewald Marischka, Klaus Müller, Irmgard Österreicher, Christian Pronay, Winfried Ritschel, Tilmann Schönmayr, Brigitta Schwarz, Christine Stranner, Franz Strasser, Anna Thier, Nada Vasic, Anne Walch, Elke Weilharter, Ursina Zwettler. Gemeinsam fassen sie sich an den Händen und rufen Ihnen zu: "Frohe Weihnachten und ein glückliches neues Jahr! Und bis bald bei dietheater Wien!"

dietheater Kunstlerhaus, dietheater Konzerthaus
Freiraum für Theater, Tanz und Performance
Karlplatz 5, 1010 Wien. Tel. +43/1/587 05 04
dietheater@gmx.net, http://www.dietheater.or.at/d-etheater

dietheater
Wien

19 **Promotion**
National Award Silver **Title** Deaf-and-Dumb-Promotion **Agency** Andreas Putz Textbuero **Client** Andreas Putz **Creative Director** Andreas Putz **Art Director** Günter Eder
Copywriter Andreas Putz **Designer** Günter Eder

20 **Promotion   Mailings**
National Award Silver **Title** Enverslund (Christmas Mailing 1998) **Design Studio** Büro X Design GmbH **Client** dietheater Wien **Creative Directors** Günter Eder, Andreas Putz
Art Director Günter Eder **Copywriter** Andreas Putz

Original snowflake from Enverslund, the residence of Santa Claus.

21 **Graphic Design   Corporate Identity**
National Award Gold **Title** Lumen Eyewear **Design Studio** Studio Krauss **Client** Design Brillen Vertriebs GesmbH **Creative Director** Alexander Kellas **Art Director** Alexander Kellas
Copywriter Norbert Tomasi **Designer** R. Himmelfreund Pointner **Photographer** Gregor Ecker **Design Group** Wiener Variante

Sports eyeglasses.

22 **Graphic Design   Corporate Identity**
National Award Silver **Title** HerziLine **Agency** Lowe GGK **Client** max.mobil **Creative Director** Dr. Peter Dirnberger **Art Directors** Wolfgang Hatwieger, Iycil Bayraktar
Illustrator Iycil Bayraktar

27 Austria

23 **Packaging**
National Award Silver **Title** Der Hut (The Hat) **Entrant** Sigi Mayer **Client** The Hat, Martha Maria **Creative Director** Sigi Mayer **Art Director** Sigi Mayer **Copywriter** Sigi Mayer
Designer Sigi Mayer

belgium

BEL
GIUM

1 **Nomination   Print Advertising   Newspaper Advertising**
National Award Gold **Title** Pig/Atomium/Viagra **Agency** GV/Company **Client** De Morgen **Creative Director** Bruno Vanspauwen **Art Director** Jan De Jonghe **Copywriter** Eric Debaene
Typographer Danny Jacquemin **Account Executives** Peter Verbiest, Inez De Pooter **Illustrator** Alain Biltereyst **Photographers** Jean-François De Witte, Stock , Pixco
Advertising Manager Koen Clement

1) The Pig. They've cracked the genetic codes. But who knows what the long term effects will be? It's a pig of a question. In De Morgen, you'll find all the latest information about it. Independent and without manipulation. Are you still with us? 2) The Atomium. The Earth is warming up. The ice-caps are melting. Water levels are rising. This has led to a flood of questions. De Morgen channels all the latest information for you. Independently and straight from the source. Are you still with us? 3) Viagra. Health is a market. With a stall for every complaint and a pill for every whim. But is everything that is medically feasible, also ethically justifiable? De Morgen dares to ask sound questions about this. Are you still with us?

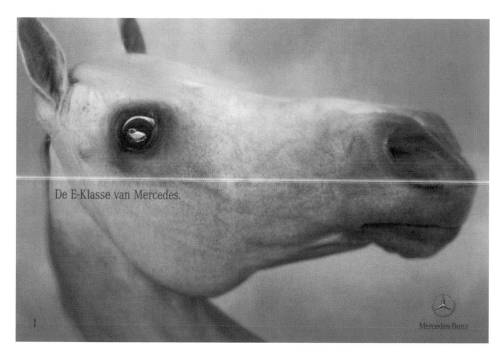

De E-Klasse van Mercedes.

2   **Nomination**   **Print Advertising**   **Magazine Advertising**
National Award Silver   **Title** Horse   **Agency** LDV/Partners   **Client** Mercedes-Benz   **Creative Director** Werner Van Reck   **Art Directors** Paul Popelier, Werner Van Reck
Copywriter Paul Van Oevelen   **Account Executives** Colette Pauwels, Beatrice Van Hool   **Photographer** Christophe Gilbert   **Advertising Managers** Marc Badde, Yves Callebaut

The Mercedes-Benz E-Class.

3   **Nomination**   **Print Advertising**   **Magazine Advertising**
National Award Silver   **Title** Haag/Wasdraad   **Agency** Duval Guillaume   **Client** BOIC   **Creative Director** Guillaume Van der Stighelen   **Art Director** Philippe De Ceuster
Copywriter Jens Mortier   **Typographer** Philippe De Ceuster   **Account Executive** Isabel Peeters   **Photographer** Koen Demuynck   **Advertising Manager** Piet Moons

Behind every Olympic champion, there's an Olympic family.

MÉGANE CABRIO

Regardez à gauche.
Regardez à droite.
Bref, comparez.

4 **Nomination   Posters   Poster Advertising**
National Award Gold **Title** Megane Cabriolet **Agency** Publicis **Client** Renault Belgique Luxembourg **Creative Director** Marco Calant **Art Director** Claude Huegaerts
Copywriter Christophe Gelder **Account Executives** Jean-Paul Dirick, Madeleine Leclercq **Photographer** Pascal Habousha **Advertising Manager** Xavier Laporta

Megane convertible.

5 **Nomination   Posters   Poster Advertising**
National Award Silver **Title** Comparez (Vespasius) **Agency** DDB **Client** Crédit Lyonnais Belgium **Creative Director** Michel De Lauw **Art Directors** Anka Cogen, Natacha Manco
Copywriters Anka Cogen, Guido Vastesaeger **Typographer** Anka Cogen **Account Executive** Wilfried De Becker **Advertising Managers** Yves Delacollette, Jean-Luc Crespin

Look to the left. Look to the right. And compare. Credit Lyonnais Belgium. You are not like everybody and so much the better.

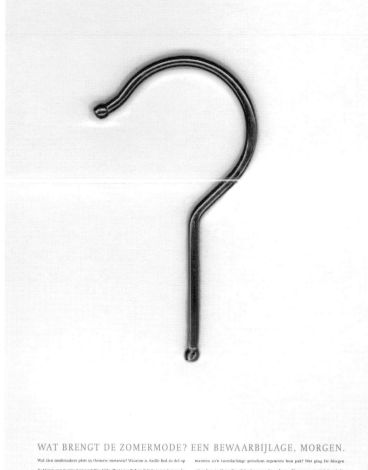

WAT BRENGT DE ZOMERMODE? EEN BEWAARBIJLAGE, MORGEN.

Wat zien modemakers plots in Oosterse motieven? Waarom is Axelle Red zo dol op de kleren van Carine Lauwers? Hoe kijkt illustrator Ruben Toledo tegen het modewereldje aan? Waarom vindt Martin Margiela dat armgaten niet opzij hoeven te zitten? Wat zijn de voordelen van de broek met één pijp, volgens Jeremy Scott? Waarom hebben mannen zo'n tweeslachtige gevoelens tegenover hun pak? Wat ging De Morgen uitspoken in Hong Kong? En hoe geraakt u daar zelf, zomaar gratis? Op al die vragen krijgt u morgen een antwoord, in onze 52 pagina's dikke modebijlage. Sla ze dus zeker aan de haak.

WIN EEN REIS VOOR 2 PERSONEN NAAR HONG KONG. *De* **Morgen** ONAFHANKELIJK DAGBLAD

6

6 **Print Advertising   Newspaper Advertising**
National Award Gold **Title** Mode Special **Agency** GV/Company **Client** De Morgen **Creative Director** Bruno Vanspauwen **Art Director** Jan De Jonghe **Copywriter** Eric Debaene
Typographer Danny Jacquemin **Account Executives** Peter Verbiest, Inez De Pooter **Advertising Manager** Koen Clement

What brings us the fashion this summer? A special supplement.

7 **Print Advertising   Newspaper Advertising**
National Award Silver **Title** Aapje/Tongzoen/Vrienden/Blinddoek/Thermisch Pak **Agency** LDV/Partners **Client** Virus (Het Nieuwsblad) **Creative Director** Werner Van Reck
Art Director Ivan Moons **Copywriter** Stef Selfslagh **Account Executive** Petra De Roos **Illustrator** Tom Hautekiet **Advertising Managers** Wouter Van Cauwenberghe, Heidi Brepoels

1) Virus is not spread by weird jungle monkeys but by news vendors of good standing, both male and female. 2) Virus is not transmitted through intimate contact but through money, preferably the right change (1x20fr, 2x5fr). 3) A carrier of Virus is not turned away nor put in quarantine. As you see, carrying virus is socially accepted. 4) The Anti-Virus. Only complete darkness protects one against the signals emitted by Virus. 5) If you don't want to expose yourself to Virus, all you have to do is not buy a newspaper on Thursday. Wearing thermal clothes is therefore ridiculous (see illustration). Virus. The Thursday supplement for the young in Het Nieuwsblad and De Gentenaar.

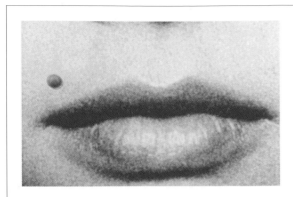

SCHOONHEIDSINSTITUUT ESTHÉ IS VERHUISD NAAR PARKLAAN 56, SINT-NIKLAAS. 777 71 16

Kom eens kijken naar wat veranderd is en wat hetzelfde gebleven is. De magic touch bijvoorbeeld.

esthé

8

9

8   **Print Advertising   Newspaper Advertising**
National Award Silver **Title** Tâche de Beauté **Agency** Peter Aerts **Client** Esthé **Art Director** Peter Aerts **Copywriter** Peter Aerts **Typographer** Peter Aerts
Advertising Manager Marielle Depaepe

Beauty salon esthé has moved to Parklane 56. Come and have a look at what has changed and what hasn't. The magic touch for example.

9   **Print Advertising   Magazine Advertising**
National Award Gold **Title** Spiderman/Postman/Taximan **Agency** TBWA **Client** Coleman **Creative Director** Andre Rysman **Art Director** Jan Macken **Copywriters** Frank Marinus,
Paul Van Oevelen **Typographers** Raf Warson, Annick Planquart **Account Executive** Koen Van Hulle **Photographer** Peter De Mulder **Advertising Manager** Nick Davies

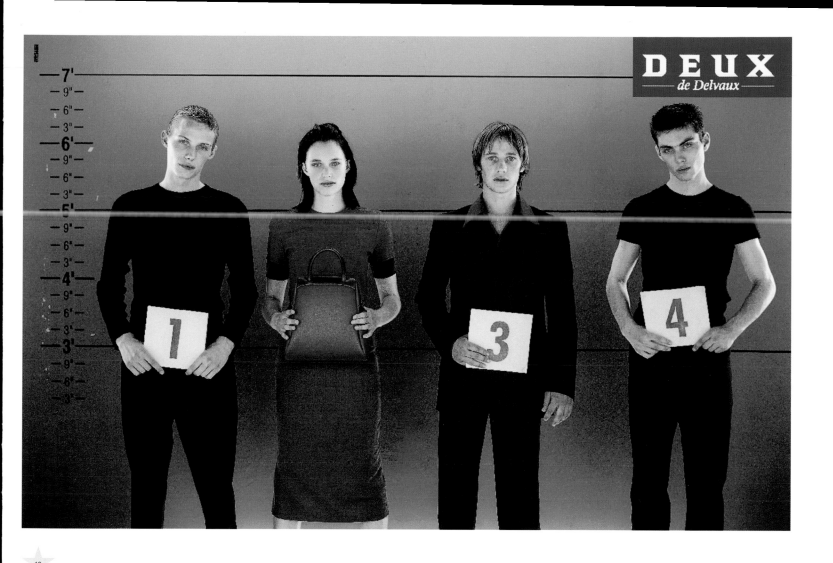

Le Meilleur de la Publicité Belge (1987-1998)

EXPOSITION AUX HALLES DE SCHAERBEEK DU 16 AU 25/10 DE 10 À 18H.

10 **Print Advertising   Magazine Advertising**
National Award Gold **Title** Deux **Agency** Kadratura **Client** Delvaux **Creative Director** Michel Mergaerts **Art Director** Sophie Norman **Copywriter** Jean-Paul Lefebvre
Account Executive Martine Cosyns **Photographer** Alain Richard **Advertising Manager** François Schwennicke

TWO of Delvaux.

11 **Print Advertising   Trade Advertising**
National Award Gold **Title** Caviar **Agency** Publicis **Client** Creative Club of Belgium **Creative Director** Marco Calant **Art Director** Jean-Marc Wachsmann **Copywriter** Gilles De Bruyere
Photographer Xavier Harcq **Advertising Manager** Siglinda Paquay

CCB Exhibition: The best of Belgian advertising 1987-1998.

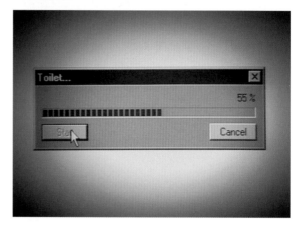

12

13

12 **Print Advertising   Trade Advertising**
National Award Gold **Title** Bic/VAB/Mestdagh **Agency** Air **Client** Mobistar **Creative Directors** Anouk Sendrowicz, Eric Hollander **Art Directors** Marc Thomasset, Pieter De Lange
Copywriters Jo De Boeck, Veronique Sels **Typographers** Anouk Sendrowicz, Joelle Hoen **Account Executive** Isabelle Moulart **Illustrator** Alain Biltereyst **Photographer** Frank Uyttenhove
Advertising Managers Antonine Seynaeve, Chris Van Roey

Bic: Bic signed with Mobistar. VAB: Mobistar helps the helpers on the road. Mestdagh: Mestdagh took a fresh start with Mobistar.

13 **TV & Cinema Advertising   Television Commercial**
National Award Gold **Title** Virtual Toilet **Agency** GV/Company **Client** De Morgen **Creative Director** Bruno Vanspauwen **Art Director** Jan De Jonghe **Copywriter** Eric Debaene
Typographer Danny Jacquemin **Account Executives** Peter Verbiest, Inez De Pooter **Production Company** Latcho Drom **Film Producer** Leila Fisher **Film Director** Raf Wathion
Film Photographer Raf Wathion **Advertising Manager** Koen Clement

A cursor selects the menu "Go to" on a computer screen and chooses the option "Toilet". What follows is a virtual "leak", the shaking of the last drop included. A super appears with the De Morgen logo and the pay off "Are you still with us?". Whereafter the user can choose a deodorant.

14

15

14 **TV & Cinema Advertising   Television Commercial**
National Award Gold **Title** Pleasure Boat/Mime/Anonymous Man **Agency** Duval Guillaume **Client** Gemeentekrediet **Creative Director** Guillaume Van der Stighelen
Art Director Alain Janssens **Copywriters** Frank Van Passel, Jean-Charles Della Faille **Account Executives** Isabel Peeters, Catherine Hamers **Production Company** Roses are Blue
Film Producer Marc Van Buggenhout **Film Directors** Frank Van Passel, Ivan Goldschmidt **Advertising Managers** Staf Helbig, Dirk Schyvinck, Bert Denis

A mortgage without going to Credit Communal, just isn't credible. We'll be your bank.

15 **TV & Cinema Advertising   Television Commercial**
National Award Silver **Title** A Sniff Movie **Agency** VVL/BBDO **Client** Passendale **Creative Director** Willy Coppens **Art Director** Peter Aerts **Copywriter** Willem De Geyndt
Account Executives Ann Lovenweent, Carola Michiels **Production Company** Latcho Drom **Film Producer** Myriam Maes **Film Director** Stef Viaene **Film Photographer** Florent Herry
Music Director Look & Listen **Advertising Manager** Herbert Coppens

A little mouse gets up on its hind feet and sniffs. In the meantime we hear a strange scraping sound. The mouse goes back on its four feet and suddenly stands up again. The reason for this strange behaviour is a pack of Passendale cheese that is being opened and closed, opened and closed, hence the scraping sound. Passensale. Now in a reseable pack.

16

17

16 **TV & Cinema Advertising   Television Commercial**
National Award Silver **Title** McRib/Potato/Kung Fu **Agency** Leo Burnett Brussels **Client** McDonald's **Creative Director** Joost Hulsbosch **Art Director** Joost Hulsbosch
Copywriter Jean-Luc Soille **Account Executive** Stephane Buisseret **Production Company** Banana Split **Film Producer** Jean-Luc Van Damme **Film Director** Annemie Van de Putte
Advertising Manager Carl Gypens

17 **TV & Cinema Advertising   Cinema Commercial**
National Award Gold & Diamond **Title** De Technieker **Agency** LDV/Partners **Client** Job@/De Personeelsgids **Creative Director** Werner Van Reck **Art Director** Ivan Moons
Copywriter Stef Selfslagh **Account Executive** Colette Pauwels **Production Company** The Chain Gang **Film Producers** Koen Brandt, Stef Selfslagh, Ivan Moons **Film Directors** Koen Brandt,
Stef Selfslagh, Ivan Moons **Music Director** Kristiaan Debusscher **Advertising Managers** Jos Vandersmissen, Geert Van Droogenbroeck

This commercial only ran in movie theatres, right after the other commercials, and thus just before the film. The screen is dark when a male voice starts talking through the speaker system.
"Ladies and gentlemen, good evening. I'm your film operator. Er...you can't see me because I'm up here, behind the window. Allow me to...er...say a few words...before starting the reel. This is
the last film I'll ever run for you. And then I quit. I...er...just wanted to say that I've had a wonderful time here, and that...er...I hope you'll enjoy my last movie. Thank you." Total silence during a few
seconds, after which, the following appears on the screen: "One day you'll find the job of a lifetime. And then of course you're gone." The commercial ends with the text: "De Personeelsgids.
Get the best out of it."

18 **TV & Cinema Advertising   Public Service/Charity (TV)**
National Award Gold **Title** Azalea **Agency** GV/Company **Client** Kom op tegen kanker (Fight Against Cancer) **Creative Director** Bruno Vanspauwen **Art Director** Stijn Gansemans
Copywriter Karel De Jonghe **Account Executives** Luc Perdieus, Konny Weber **Production Company** Blue Stone **Film Producer** Jean-Marc Gerbehaye **Film Directors** Jean-Marc
Gerbehaye, Stijn Gansemans **Music Directors** Bleu Nuit, Pierre Bruyns **Advertising Manager** Leo Leys

We see different herbs and their respective applications in medicine. Mint freshens the breath, camomille aids the digestion, sage relieves sore throats. The last to appear is azalea.
Azalea fights cancer. Azalea is on sale in favour of "Fight Cancer".

19 **TV & Cinema Advertising   Public Service/Charity (TV)**
National Award Silver **Title** Karaoke/Crying Little Girl **Agency** VVL/BBDO **Client** 11.11.11 - NCOS **Creative Director** Willem De Geyndt **Art Director** Peter Aerts
Copywriter Willem De Geyndt **Account Executives** Lies Debrouwere, Carola Michiels **Production Company** ACE **Radio Production Company** Doctor Swing
Producer Myriam Maes **Film Directors** Catherine Leterme, Peter Aerts, Doctor Swing **Music Director** Doctor Swing **Radio Director** Doctor Swing **Advertising Manager** Marleen Vos

She can cry. No wonder. 11.11.11. Fight against injustice.

Cette fois, c'est pour Porsche.

mobistar | business solutions | cette fois, c'est pour vous.

Cette fois, c'est pour Royal Canin.

mobistar | business solutions | cette fois, c'est pour vous.

Chez M&M's, on a choisi Mobistar.

mobistar | business solutions

Chez Panzani, on a choisi Mobistar.

mobistar | business solutions

 20

 21

20 **Posters   Poster Advertising**
National Award Gold **Title** Porsche/Royal Canin/M&M's/Panzani **Agency** Air **Client** Mobistar **Creative Directors** Anouk Sendrowicz, Eric Hollander **Art Directors** Steven de Vreese, Marc Thomasset **Copywriters** Jo De Boeck, Veronique Sels **Typographers** Anouk Sendrowicz, Joelle Hoen **Account Executive** Isabelle Moulart **Photographers** Frank Uyttenhove, Charles Van Hoorick **Advertising Managers** Antonine Seynaeve, Chris Van Roey

Porsche: Porsche drives Mobistar. Royal Canin: At Royal Canin, Mobistar is king. M&Ms: M&Ms melt for Mobistar. Panzani: At Panzani, they worship Mobistar.

21 **Posters   Poster Advertising**
National Award Silver **Title** Desert/Diving/Cruise **Agency** Publicis **Client** Egyptian Tourist Authority **Creative Director** Marco Calant **Art Director** Eric Jamez **Copywriter** Fabrice Storti **Typographer** Eric Jamez **Account Executives** Carine Yvanoff, Eric Vereecke **Advertising Manager** Cherif Abdol Rhaman

Amaze your eyes ("eyes" as a pictogram).

Gezocht: geen ervaring.

Creyf's Interim biedt afgestudeerden graag
een eerste werkervaring aan.

Creyf's ☺ Interim

25 **Promotion**
National Award Silver **Title** Gift for Life **Agency** Saatchi & Saatchi **Client** Euroliver Foundation **Creative Director** Danny Pauwels **Art Director** Marie-Laure Cliquennois
Copywriter Gregory Ginterdaele **Typographer** Marie-Laure Cliquennois **Account Executive** Frederic Jadinon **Advertising Manager** Herman Tob

26 **Promotion**
National Award Gold **Title** Peugeot 206 - bâches **Agency** Palmares **Client** Peugeot **Creative Director** Hugues Vanden Steen **Art Director** Jean-François Dooms
Copywriters Hugues Vanden Steen, Pascal Witmeur **Account Executive** Celine Houbion **Advertising Managers** Rene Cromphout, Eric Elsen

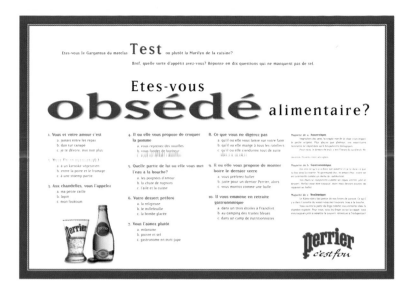

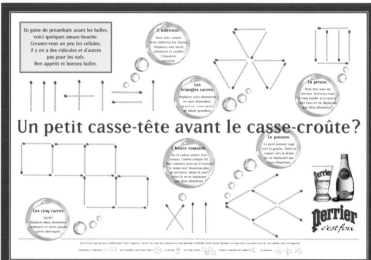

27 **Promotion   Mailings**
National Award Silver **Title** Medievil **Agency** TBWA **Client** Sony Playstation **Creative Director** Andre Rysman **Art Director** Koen Demare **Copywriter** Koen Demare
Account Executive Koen Van Hulle **Graphic Designer** Raf Warson **Photographer** Pascal Habousha **Advertising Managers** Ronny Hoekman, Tom Robberechts

Gloomy dealer mailing to promote Medievil, a new game full of hostile skeletons and dark humour.

28 **Promotion**
National Award Silver **Title** Test/Matches **Agency** Ogilvy & Mather **Client** Perrier **Creative Director** Mark Hilltout **Art Director** Geert Joostens **Copywriter** Olivier Roland
Typographer Geert Joostens **Account Executive** David Grunewald **Photographer** Filip Van Zieleghem **Advertising Managers** Jacques Nijskens, Nathalie Puchevrier

Test: Are you a foodaholic? Matches: Before the food, some food for thought.

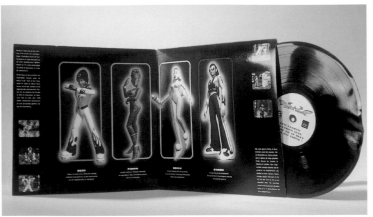

29

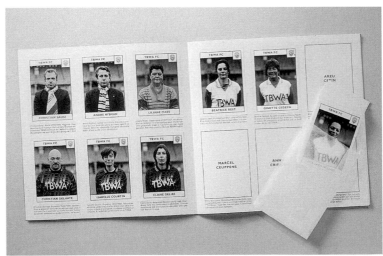

30

29 Promotion   Mailings
National Award Gold   **Title** Bust A Groove   **Agency** TBWA   **Client** Sony PlayStation   **Creative Director** Andre Rysman   **Art Director** Koen Demare   **Copywriter** Koen Demare
Account Executive Koen Van Hulle   **Graphic Designer** Raf Warson   **Advertising Managers** Ronny Hoekman, Tom Robberechts

Disco-style mailing to promote Bustagroove, a new interactive dance game.

30 Promotion   Mailings
National Award Silver   **Title** TBWA FC   **Agency** TBWA   **Client** Self promotional   **Creative Director** André Rysman   **Advertising Agency** Creative department TBWA
Copywriter Creative department TBWA

Christmas card, starring the agency people as football players.

GERMANY

deutschland

Angelschnüre von **SILSTAR**

1 **Gold Award   Print Advertising   Trade Advertising**
National Award Silver **Title** Silstar ad Vanished **Agency** Springer & Jacoby Werbung GmbH **Client** Silstar **Creative Directors** Torsten Rieken, Jan Ritter **Art Director** Torsten Rieken
Copywriter Jan Ritter **Photographer** Gerd George

Fishing lines from Silstar.

2   **Gold Award   TV & Cinema Advertising   Public Service/Charity (TV)**
National Award Gold **Title** Handicap (Titanic) **Production Company** Hope & Glory Commercials GmbH **Client** Initiative Against Right Wing Violence **Copywriters** Martin Sonneborn,
Benjamin Schiffner **Film Director** Caspar-Jan Hogerzeil **Director of Photography** Eva Fleig

...a short film about a pitiable minority of our society, showing how hard everyday life of Nazis can be...

3 Gold Award   Graphic Design   Annual Reports, Catalogues, Calendars, Compact Disks & Record Sleeves etc
National Award Gold **Title** Calendar Mindestens Haltbar bis......... **Entrant** Verlag Hermann Schmidt Mainz **Client** Verlag Hermann Schmidt Mainz **Creative Director** Juli Gudehus
Art Director Juli Gudehus **Designer** Juli Gudehus **Photographer** Alistar Overbruck

Calendar. Best before end of 2000.

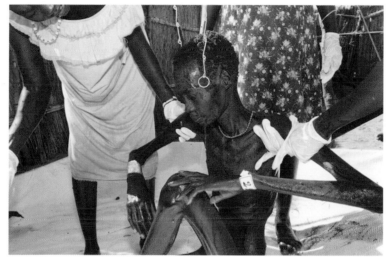

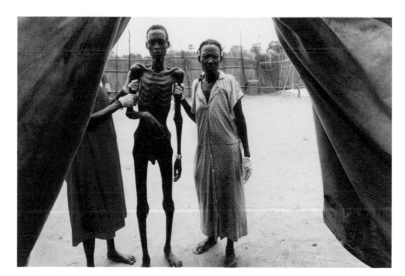

4 **Gold Award   Illustration & Photography   Photography**
National Award Silver **Title** Southern Sudan **Agency** Gruner + Jahr AG & Co. **Art Director** Wolfgang Behnken **Photographer** Hans-Jürgen Burkard

Southern Sudan. Refugee Camp of Aigip. Famine victims in a camp of "Médicins Sans Frontières".

5

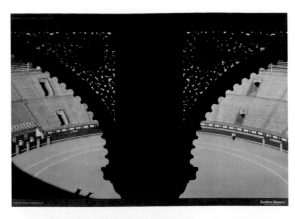

 6

5 **Nomination** **Print Advertising** **Newspaper Advertising**
National Award Silver **Title** FAZ Campaign. There is always a clever mind behind it **Agency** Scholz & Friends Berlin **Client** Frankfurter Allgemeine Zeitung GmbH
Creative Director Sebastian Turner **Art Director** Petra Reichenbach **Copywriter** Sebastian Turner **Graphic artists** Ronald Liedmeier, Frank Melzer **Photographer** Alfred Seiland
Post production Hans-Jürgen Gaeltzner

1) "Jupp Heynckes" ousted German-born soccer coach of Real Madrid, features the traditional logo of the newspaper Frankfurter Allgemeine Zeitung. 2) "Rudolph Augstein" publisher of the newsweekly "Spiegel" (English: Mirror), features the traditional logo of the newspaper Frankfurter Allgemeine Zeitung in the Hall of Mirrors at the Palace of Versailles (Note: the picture is a mirror image). 3) "Ricardo Diez Hochleitner" president of the Club of Rome, features the traditional logo of the newspaper Frankfurter Allgemeine Zeitung. The Club of Rome is warning that the world may become a desert.

6 **Nomination** **Print Advertising** **Magazine Advertising**
National Award Silver **Title** Silstar ad Vanished **Agency** Springer & Jacoby Werbung GmbH **Client** Silstar **Creative Director** Torsten Rieken, Jan Ritter **Art Director** Torsten Rieken
Copywriter Jan Ritter **Photographer** Gerd George

Fishing Lines from Silstar.

7 **Nomination   Print Advertising   Magazine Advertising**
National Award Gold   **Title** The Manager Magazine Campaign   **Agency** Springer & Jacoby Werbung GmbH   **Client** Manager Magazin Verlagsgesellschaft mbH
Creative Directors Arno Lindemann, Stefan Meske, André Aimaq   **Art Director** Paul Holcmann   **Copywriter** Amir Kassaei   **Photographer** Jo Jankowski

"Tycoon" 1) 1973: Oil Crisis. 2) 1987: Wall Street Crash. 3) 1998: Dispute with the Chairman. Manager Magazine. Business - The Inside Story. "Elevator" 1) If the share price drops, he'll be the Head of Trading. 2) If the share price rises, he'll be Head of Trading. 3) The Head of Trading. Manager Magazine. Business - The Inside Story. "Interview" 1) Thanks to him the group is in the black. 2) Thanks to him nobody knows it's really in the red. Manager Magazine. Business - The Inside Story.

8 **Nomination   Print Advertising   Magazine Advertising**
National Award Silver   **Title** Bild Campaign   **Agency** JvM Werbeagentur GmbH   **Client** Axel Springer Verlag AG   **Creative Director** Doerte Spengler   **Art Directors** Roland Schwarz,
Mathias Massa   **Copywriter** Michael Ohanian   **Photographers** Andreas Doria, Action Press, Corbis Bettmann

Anyone with something important to say avoids long sentences.

Der CDI-Diesel.
Ein Diesel wie kein Diesel.

Mercedes-Benz
Die Zukunft des Automobils.

9 **Nomination**   **Print Advertising**   **Trade Advertising**
National Award Silver **Title** Götze ad, Got Lost **Agency** Springer & Jacoby Werbung GmbH **Client** Dr. Götze Land und Karte (maps) **Creative Director** S&J Junior School
Art Director Thomas Knobloch **Copywriter** Peter Jooss

10 **Nomination**   **TV & Cinema Advertising**   **Television Commercial**
National Award Gold **Title** Silence **Agency** Springer & Jacoby Werbung GmbH **Client** DaimlerChrysler AG **Creative Directors** Torsten Rieken, Jan Ritter **Art Director** Eric Urmetzer
Copywriter Reinhard Crasemann **Agency Producer** Natascha Teidler **Film Director** Fabrice Carazo **Production Company** Markenfilm GmbH & Co.

An elderly man with a hearing aid is picked up by his son in a new Mercedes. He sits in the car and hears nothing. Increasing the volume on his hearing aid, he still can't hear anything. Until his son speaks. The hearing aid whistles loudly. The CDI Diesel. A diesel like no other.

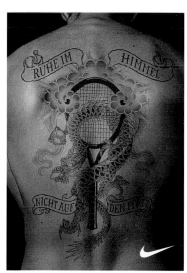

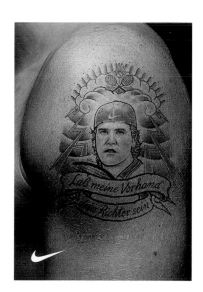

11 **Nomination   TV & Cinema Advertising   Television Commercial**
National Award Silver **Title** Interviews **Agency** JvM Werbeagentur GmbH **Client** Axel Springer Verlag AG **Creative Directors** Doerte Spengler, Stefan Meske **Art Director** Thomas Pakull
Copywriter Michael Ohanian **Agency Producer** Britta Wolgast **Production Company** Chips & Clips

Sports interviews are great: you learn so much about training methods, self motivation and all those personal feuds. Or perhaps, not as the BILD image-films so clearly suggest. Not to worry, because at the end of the day, everything worth knowing appears in BILD.

12 **Nomination   Posters   Poster Advertising**
National Award Silver **Title** Nike Eurocard Open Tattoo Campaign **Agency** Wieden & Kennedy Amsterdam **Client** Nike Germany **Creative Directors** Glenn Cole, Robert Nakata
Art Director Robert Nakata **Copywriters** Tim Wolfe, Marc Wirbeleit **Photographer** Jasper Wiedeman **Illustrator (Tattoo Artist)** Rob Admiraal

"Heart Tattoo". Love thy neighbour but obliterate his ground game. "Dragon Tattoo". Rest in heaven not in the court. "Player 1". Haas: My forehand will be thy judge.

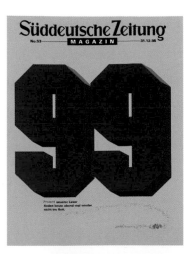

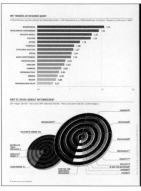

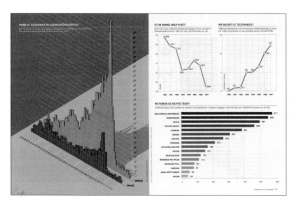

13 **Nomination** **Editorial**
National Award Silver **Title** Magazine 99% **Publisher** Magazinverlagsges. Süddeutsche Zeitung mbH **Art Director** Petra Langhammer **Designers** Petra Langhammer, Martin Stallmann, Anne Blaschke, Wilhelm Raffelsberger

99% (of our readers won't find their bed tonight. The statistics issue).

14 **Nomination** **Editorial**
National Award Silver **Title** Essen kann so schön sein **Publisher** Jetzt - Magazine **Client** Süddeutscher Verlag **Art Director** Markus Rindermann **Copywriter** Philip Reichardt **Designer** Markus Rindermann **Photographer** Oliver Spiess

Food can be so beautiful.

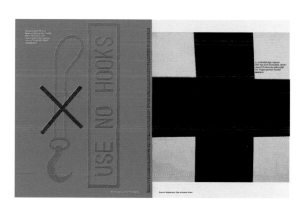

15 **Nomination   Editorial**
National Award Silver   **Title** Rome is far   **Publisher** Die Woche Zeitungsverlag   **Art Director** Dirk Linke   **Designers** Armin Ogris, Andreas Schomberg, Stefan Semrau, Jessica Winter, Reinhard Schulz-Schaeffer, Florian Pöhl   **Photographer** Thomas Müller

16 **Nomination   Editorial**
National Award Silver   **Title** A Sign (There is only one shape in the world, that signifies so much)   **Publisher** Magazinverlagsges. Süddeutsche Zeitung mbH   **Art Director** Markus Rasp
Designer Petra Schlie   **Photographers** Yukio Futagawa, Neil Leifer, Mona Giulini, Bruce Roberts, Margaret Bourke-White, Andreas Serrano, Kasimir Malewitsch

17 Nomination   Editorial
National Award Silver **Title** Die Götter müssen verrückt sein **Publisher** Magazinverlagsges. Süddeutsche Zeitung mbH **Art Director** Markus Rasp **Copywriter** Michael Cornelius
Photographer Christopher Thomas

The Gods must be crazy: If Leprosy is the punishment from Heaven, What does Hell look like? A visit in Katmandu.

18 Nomination   Editorial
National Award Silver **Title** Welcome to the Berliner Republic **Publisher** Die Woche Zeitungsverlag **Art Director** Dirk Linke **Designers** Andreas Schomberg, Armin Ogris,
Stefan Semrau, Jessica Winter, Reinhard Schulz-Schaeffer, Florian Pöhl

19 **Nomination   Editorial**
National Award Silver **Title** The Palestinians **Publisher** Gruner + Jahr AG & Co. **Client** Stern **Art Director** Wolfgang Behnken **Designer** Andreas Fischer **Photographer** Kai Wiedenhöfer

They grow up with hate and violence in miserable refugee camps. The young PLO fighters want to take revenge on the Israeli occupants. They still long for Palestine.
1) People in a ghetto. 2) We are the revenge. 3) Peace is still a long way.

20 **Nomination   Illustration & Photography   Photography**
National Award Silver **Title** There is always a clever mind behind it **Agency** Scholz & Friends Berlin **Client** Frankfurter Allgemeine Zeitung GmbH **Creative Director** Sebastian Turner
Art Director Petra Reichenbach **Copywriter** Sebastian Turner **Graphic Artists** Ronald Liedmeier, Frank Melzer **Photographer** Alfred Seiland **Post Production** Hans-Jürgen Gaeltzner

★ 21

★ 22

21 Print Advertising   Newspaper Advertising
National Award Silver **Title** Hypovereinsbank Launch Campaign **Agency** Wieden & Kennedy Amsterdam **Client** HypoVereinsbank, Germany **Creative Directors** Jon Matthews, John Boiler
Art Directors Irene Kugelmann, Frank Hahn **Copywriters** Giles Montgomery, Marc Wirbeleit **Photographers** Paul Wetherell, Mark Borthwick

1) "All my Life". I've worked hard to earn money. Now it's time someone else worked hard figuring out where to invest that money. The job's open. Interested? You live. We'll take care of the details.
HypoVereinsbank. 2) "Lotto". I expect to win the lottery any time soon. I can feel it. But I promise it won't change me. I'll still be completely hopeless with money. You live. We'll take care of the
details. HypoVereinsbank. 3) "Stock Exchange". I know something about the stock market. But I don't know where the top 5 European Blue Chips are placed right now. I'm a businesswoman,
not a game show candidate. You live. We'll take care of the details. HypoVereinsbank.

22 Print Advertising   Magazine Advertising
National Award Silver **Title** Jump! ad Rabbit **Agency** TBWA Frankfurt **Client** Rhönsprudel **Creative Director** Rainer Bollmann **Art Directors** Susanne Graf, Mirjam Hasch
Copywriter Tommy Mayer **Photographer** M. Tollhopf

23 **Print Advertising   Magazine Advertising**
National Award Silver **Title** FAZ Campaign. There is always a clever mind behind it **Agency** Scholz & Friends Berlin **Client** Frankfurter Allgemeine Zeitung GmbH
Creative Director Sebastian Turner **Art Director** Petra Reichenbach **Copywriter** Sebastian Turner **Graphic Artists** Ronald Liedmeier, Frank Melzer **Photographer** Alfred Seiland
Post Production Hans-Jürgen Gaeltzner

1) "Albert Mangelsdorff" trumpet player, features the traditional logo of the newspaper Frankfurter Allgemeine Zeitung at the crumbling walls in Jerico, the biblical city that was destroyed by trumpets. 2) "Joschka Fischer" leader of the Green Party, features the traditional logo of the newspaper Frankfurter Allgemeine Zeitung in a greenhouse in Bonn. 3) "Hans Magnus Enzenberger" Germany's internationally reknown author, features the traditional logo of the newspaper Frankfurter Allgemeine Zeitung at the library of Trinity College in Dublin.

24 **Print Advertising   Magazine Advertising**
National Award Gold **Title** Spiegel ad Dürer's Praying Hands **Agency** Springer & Jacoby Werbung GmbH **Client** Spiegel Verlag GmbH **Creative Directors** Kurt Georg Dieckert, Stefan Schmidt
Art Directors Kathrin Berger, Christina Petrich **Copywriter** Thomas Chudalla **Illustrator** Warren Madill **Agency (Design Group)** Meikle John

SPIEGEL readers know more.

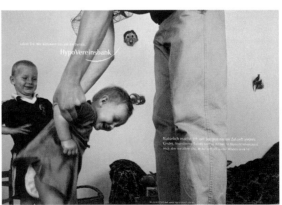

25 **Print Advertising   Magazine Advertising**
National Award Silver **Title** Lufthansa Campaign. Brand Mission **Agency** Springer & Jacoby Werbung GmbH **Client** Deutsche Lufthansa AG **Creative Directors** Hans-Jürgen Lewandowski,
André Aimaq **Art Directors** Jan Rexhausen, Patricia Längerer **Copywriters** Patricia Längerer, Jan Rexhausen, T. Wildberger, Hans-Jürgen Lewandowski, André Aimaq **Designer** Antje Hedde
Photographers P. Gehrke, P. Seaward, F. Reidenbach, C. Morlinghaus, W. Klein **Art Buying** T. Braune **Graphic Artists** K. Rambaum, A. Hartwig

26 **Print Advertising   Magazine Advertising**
National Award Gold **Title** HypoVereinsbank Campaign **Agency** Wieden & Kennedy Amsterdam **Client** HypoVereinsbank, Germany **Creative Directors** Jon Matthews, John Boiler
Art Directors Irene Kugelmann, Frank Hahn **Copywriters** Giles Montgomery, Marc Wirbeleit **Photographers** Paul Wetherell, Mark Borthwick

1) "Small Business". I run a small business. When my clients don't pay their bills on time I lose sleep. When I lose sleep I can't dream about the future of my business. Can anybody help me get
more sleep? You Live. We'll take care of the details. HypoVereinsbank. 2) "Baby". Naturally I'm concerned about my child's future, investment funds and...whatever. But at the moment I'm just
concerned with one thing: how do I know which is the front of the nappy? You Live. We'll take care of the details. HypoVereinsbank.

27

28

27 TV & Cinema Advertising   Television Commercial
National Award Silver **Title** Coca Cola TV-Campaign **Production Company** Jo! Schmid Filmproduktion GmbH **Client** Coca Cola GmbH Essen **Creative Director** Jon Matthews
Art Director Stephan Auer **Agency Producer** Meike Wetzstein **Film Director** Martin Schmid **Director of Photography** Franz Lustig **Agency** Wieden & Kennedy

"Monk". First we see Father Burkhard wearing his monk cowl and holding a football in his arms. Some people describe the monks behaviour as very unusual, because sometimes he is like two persons in one. On one side he is a normal monk with all his duties, but on the other side he interrupts marriages to go to watch the football match of his favourite team and drinks Coca Cola. "Music Professor". A music professor sits in a lecture hall and gives a lecture about all the different rituals of football fans. He talks about the masks, the dancing, the singing and the certain drink, the Coke, that those special fans take. In between the fans are shown with their mask faces, the way they sing and dance and the way they act and drink Coca Cola. "Gnomes". The different members of a football fan club are talking about their unusual hobby. They disguise themselves as gnomes before they to go to matches and that in the beginning everybody poked fun at them but now it is completely normal for everybody to see the gnomes. Then all of them are shown standing in a crowd in a stadium disguised as gnomes, drinking Coca Cola, watching the match and firing up their team.

28 TV & Cinema Advertising   Television Commercial
National Award Silver **Title** Flame **Agency** KNSK, BBDO Werbeagentur **Client** o. tel. o communications GmbH & Co. **Creative Directors** Ulrike Wegert, Christian Traut
Art Director Tim Krink **Copywriter** Ulrike Wegert **Agency Producers** Tim Krink, Ulrike Wegert **Film Director** Tony Kaye **Production Company** Petersen Naumann

A plumpish teenager is dancing in her room. She is gazing adoringly at the photo of a very good looking boy. After a while she can't stand it any longer, she gets her telephone and dials a number. Being excited she's waiting for somebody to pick up the phone. When hearing a boy saying "Hello?" she hangs up the phone and dances through her room like being in heaven. Later she's going to repeat the procedure. "What a good thing that o.tel.o is fair and charges by the second and not by the number. o.tel.o. For a better understanding.

29 Posters   Poster Advertising
National Award Gold **Title** Stilwerk: Calorie/Apple/Dog **Agency** JvM Werbeagentur GmbH **Client** Stilwerk **Creative Director** Mike Ries **Art Director** Uli Guertler
Photographer Kai Uwe Gundlach **Copywriter** Oliver Kessler

1) Such a beautiful home for a calorie. What's yours like? 2) Such a beautiful home for a worm. What's yours like? 3) Such a beautiful home for a flea. What's yours like?

30 Posters   Public Service/Charity (P)
National Award Silver **Title** Vultures **Agency** KNSK, BBDO Werbeagentur GmbH **Client** SPD – German Social Democratic Party **Creative Directors** Ulrike Wegert, Detlef Krüger
Art Director Andreas Geyer **Copywriter** Ulrich Zünkeler **Graphic Designers** Bettina Fuhrmann, Katrin Mielke, Silke Baltruschat

This shows former chancellor Mr. Kohl before the elections (September 1998). The vultures are already lurking above him.

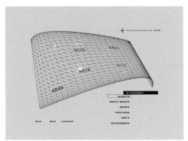

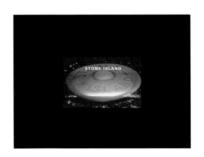

33 Promotion
 National Award Silver **Title** Görtz. The great shoe handout campaign **Agency** Springer & Jacoby Werbung GmbH **Client** Ludwig Görtz GmbH **Creative Directors** Suse Uhlenbrock, Constantin Kaloff **Art Directors** Käthe Schomburg, Britta Smyrak **Copywriter** Nuria Pizan **Designer** Antje Hedde **Graphic Artist** Katja Knoblich

10,000 odd shoes have been distributed, to which the matching shoes must be found. This was supported by a variety of advertising.

34 Interactive Media   Distributed Media (CD ROMs, DVDs etc)
 National Award Gold **Title** Stone Island No. 4 Catalogue **Studio** E **Client** Sportswear Company/Stone Island **Creative Directors** Christiane Boerdner, Marcus Gaab, Matthias Schellenberg **Photographer** Marcus Gaab

Stone Island, the very exclusive Italian research and technology oriented sportswear label has released this fourth CD-ROM catalogue. As usual, the idea beyond this interactive, totally digital (also photography and music) CD-ROM is to explore the mainstay pieces of the collection in the most innovative way, by enabling the visitor to view certain items from 360 degrees, or by zooming into microscopic scale of certain fabrics.

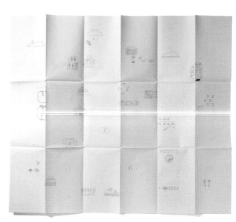

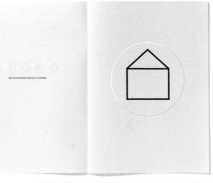

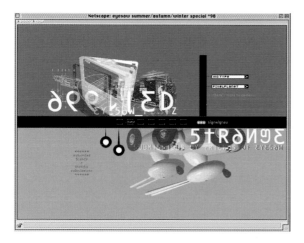

35 **Interactive Media   Internet**
National Award Silver **Title** Eyesaw Fontz - Website **Design Studio** Signalgrau Design Bureau **Client** Self promotional piece **Creative Director** Dirk Uhlenbrock **Art Director** Dirk Uhlenbrock
Copywriter Dirk Uhlenbrock **Designer** Dirk Uhlenbrock **Photographer** Dirk Uhlenbrock **Illustrator** Dirk Uhlenbrock

"Eyesaw" is a design training field and playground. It represents Signalgrau's non-commercial font faces. These were given away free to start communication, contacting the anonymous web-community. Promotion. Overview: Design for me is like building a sandcastle on the beach. You start by digging holes to get enough material for building. Then develop the first rough form, going into detail, you continue. Parts collapse and must be rebuilt. The whole thing is altering its shape during its evolution, and then its finished. The sun is shining, people go by and take notice of your work. Time after time you add some annexes and one-day you'll be the tide, wash it away and built a new one… Eyesaw is the result of typographic experiments, which started in January 1997 when first contact was made with fontographer. Eyesaw is the King of training – making a font and site keeps my fingers and brain fast and healthy - Dirk Uhlenbrock.

36 **Graphic Design   Annual Reports, Catalogues, Calendars, Compact Disks & Record Sleeves etc**
National Award Silver **Title** Cartographic Book "Mazzini/Payer" **Entrant** Almut Riebe **Art Director** Almut Riebe **Copywriter** Christoph Ransmayr **Designer** Almut Riebe **Illustrator** Almut Riebe

"Mazzini/Payer" - Cartographic book by Almut Riebe. Based on the novel "The Terrors of Ice and Darkness". Julius Payer is Commander of a polar expedition, whose members found themselves enclosed by pack ice in the year 1870, followed by two winters in "The Terrors of Ice and Darkness". Josef Mazzini is a fictional character following the tracks of this true-life story (So far the content of the novel). The notes made by Payer and other participants of the expedition ("   /Payer") are examined and arranged material Mazzini uses to form his own personal experience ("Mazzini /   ). Things experienced and those re-experienced are drawn into a map, which can be "read" (Mazzini/Payer) or be regarded as a coherent unit (the folded map included in the slipcase). Experiences and their recordings correspond to the typography: on the one hand to a copy without any obvious structure (Mazzini /   ) and in the other hand to a cartographic system (/Payer). In this system each experience is given a certain place and a significant expansion in a typographical way. The drawings serve as a map that helps to walk along sketched paths again. The numbers represent a location and referring system between each book. At the beginning of each book, a legend - as always used in cartographic works - shows the viewer/reader, the way.

37 **Graphic Design   Annual Reports, Catalogues, Calendars, Compact Disks & Record Sleeves etc**
National Award Silver **Title** Gaggenau folder. www.gaggenau.com **Agency** Rempen & Partner München **Client** Gaggenau Hausgeräte GmbH **Creative Director** Frank Lübke
Art Directors Oliver Helligrath, Ploi Malakul **Copywriters** Sascha Koller, Gerrit Schwerzel, Oliver Böttcher

Website http://www.gaggenau.com/
The objective was to design an internet - appearance describing its function in a way that would consequently represent the philosophy behind the product itself: Ultimate unison of form and function. Some kitchen appliances need a little more room to develop the desired effect.

nederland

HOLL
AND

1   **Gold Award   Promotion**
National Award Silver **Title** Bavaria Holiday Pictures Promotion **Agency** Schaeffer Wünsch Has **Client** Bavaria **Creative Directors** Lode Schaeffer, Erik Wünsch **Art Director** Lode Schaeffer
Copywriter Erik Wünsch **Typographer** Max Christoffel **Photographer** Yani **Production Companies** Borremans & Ruseler, Schaeffer Wünsch Has

And now for a Bavaria.

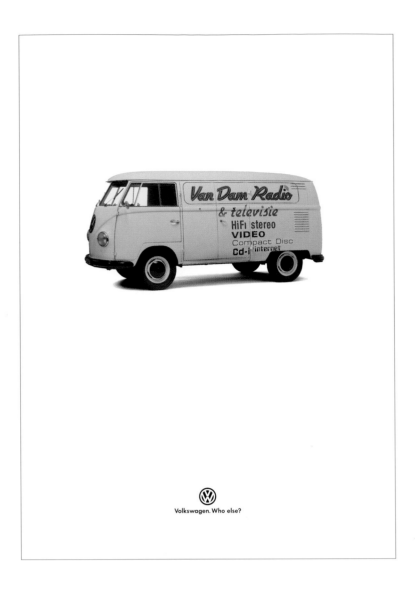

2 **Nomination** **Print Advertising** **Newspaper Advertising**
National Award Silver **Title** VW Van **Agency** Result DDB **Client** Pon's Automobielhandel bv **Creative Director** Michael Jansen **Art Director** Jeroen van Zwam **Copywriter** Marcel Hartog
Photographer Peter Boudestein **Typographers** Martin de Jong, John de Vries

3 **Nomination** **Print Advertising** **Magazine Advertising**
National Award Silver **Title** Surfer **Agency** TBWA/Campaign Company **Client** Delta Lloyd **Art Director** Diederick Hillenius **Copywriter** Poppe van Pelt **Photographer** Paul Ruigrok

...Delta Lloyd Insurance for sure.

 4

 5

It feels bigger than it is.

VW

The Lupo.

VW

Volkswagen. Who else?

4   **Nomination   TV & Cinema Advertising   Television Commercial**
National Award Gold **Title** Bridge **Agency** Result DDB **Client** Pon's Automobielhandel bv **Creative Director** Michael Jansen **Art Director** Michael Jansen **Copywriters** Marcel Hartog, Bas Engels, Zwier Veldhoen **Agency Producer** Marloes van den Berg **Film Director** Maarten Treurniet **Directors of Photography** Barry Ackroyd, Bastiaan Houtkooper, Joost van Starrenburg **Production Company** 25FPS

Volkswagen Lupo.

5   **Nomination   TV & Cinema Advertising   Television Commercial**
National Award Silver **Title** Workshop **Agency** Result DDB **Client** Pon's Automobielhandel bv **Creative Director** Michael Jansen **Art Director** Sanne Braam **Copywriter** Bas Engels **Agency Producer** Marloes van den Berg **Film Director** Rick Lenzing **Director of Photography** Steve Walker **Production Company** Cellusion Films

Volkswagen Commercial Vehicles Workshop.

6   **Nomination   TV & Cinema Advertising   Television Commercial**
National Award Gold **Title** Airport 98 **Agency** Wieden & Kennedy Amsterdam **Client** Nike International Beaverton **Creative Directors** Dan Wieden, Jon Matthews **Art Director** John Boiler
Copywriter Glenn Cole **Agency Producer** Charles Wolford **Film Director** John Woo **Production Company** A Band Apart Commercials

Faced with the boredom of waiting for a delayed flight to Paris, the Brazillian National Team plays a football game in Rio International Airport that quickly runs out of control.

7   **Nomination   TV & Cinema Advertising   Television Commercial**
National Award Silver **Title** Music in Words **Agency** KesselsKramer **Client** Oor Music Magazine **Creative Directors** Erik Kessels, Johan Kramer **Art Director** Karen Heuter
Copywriter Dave Bell **Agency Producer** Jacqueline Kouwenberg **Film Director** Brian Baderman **Director of Photography** Richard Greatex

Techno/Hip Hop/Drum 'N' Bass/Punk/R&B.

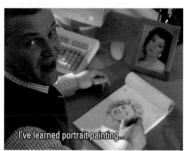

8   **Nomination   TV & Cinema Advertising   Television Commercial**
National Award Silver **Title** Internet **Agency** TBWA/Campaign Company **Client** Telfort **Art Director** Matthijs van Wensveen **Copywriter** Zwier Veldhoen **Agency Producer** Miriam Buise **Film Director** Rogier van der Ploeg **Production Company** Czar Films

Wouldn't it be easier if your Internet connection was just a little bit quicker? Telfort. A lot easier to talk with.

9   **Nomination   TV & Cinema Advertising   Television Commercial**
National Award Silver **Title** Shark **Agency** Van Walbeek Etcetera **Client** Gouden Gids **Creative Directors** Ben Imhoff, Willem van Harrewijen **Art Directors** Ben Imhoff, Michiel Neefjes **Copywriters** Rogier Mahieu, Willem van Harrewijen **Agency Producer** Annabel van Ditmar **Film Director** Matthijs van Heijningen jr **Director of Photography** Joost van Gelder **Production Company** Czar Films

Yellow Pages: two cleaners and a shark.

It feels bigger than it is.

The Lupo.

Amsterdam leest Het Parool
Nickie Nicole
Abonnee sinds januari '98

Amsterdam leest Het Parool
Özay Celikbas
Abonnee sinds juni '95

Amsterdam leest Het Parool
J. v.d. Boogaard Kool
Abonnee sinds november '93

Amsterdam leest Het Parool
Iwan Leeuwin
Abonnee sinds oktober '97

Amsterdam leest Het Parool
E. van Thijn
Abonnee sinds april '53

10 **Nomination   TV & Cinema Advertising   Cinema Commercial**
National Award Silver **Title** Courier **Agency** Result DDB **Client** Pon's Automobielhandel bv **Creative Director** Michael Jansen **Art Director** Michael Jansen **Copywriters** Marcel Hartog,
Bas Engels **Agency Producer** Marloes van den Berg **Film Director** Maarten Treurniet **Director of Photography** Barry Ackroyd, Bastiaan Houtkooper, Joost van Starrenburg
Production Company 25 FPS

Volkswagen Lupo Courier.

11 **Nomination   Illustration & Photography   Photography**
National Award Silver **Title** Amsterdam Reads Het Parool **Agency** KesselsKramer **Client** Het Parool **Creative Directors** Erik Kessels, Johan Kramer **Art Director** Erik Kessels
Copywriter Johan Kramer **Photographer** To Sang

So. Und jetzt ein Bavaria.

12

13

12 **Print Advertising   Newspaper Advertising**
   National Award Silver **Title** Derrick **Agency** Schaeffer Wünsch Has **Client** Bavaria **Creative Directors** Lode Schaeffer, Erik Wünsch **Art Director** Christien van Citters
   Copywriter J-P Nieuwerkerk **Typographer** Max Christoffel **Photographer** Raimond Wouda **Producers** Violet van der Straaten, Lex Szántó

   And now for a Bavaria.

13 **Print Advertising   Trade Advertising**
   National Award Silver **Title** Truth in Advertising **Agency** Schaeffer Wünsch Has **Client** Adformatie **Creative Directors** Lode Schaeffer, Erik Wünsch **Art Director** Christien van Citters
   Copywriter J-P Nieuwerkerk **Typographer** Max Christoffel **Photographer** Derk-Jan Gerritsen

   No junkmail/no freesheets.

14 **TV & Cinema Advertising**   **Television Commercial**
National Award Silver **Title** It's Completed **Agency** PPGH/JWT **Client** BMW Nederland bv **Creative Directors** Romke Oortwijn, Peter Hebbing **Art Director** Peter Hebbing
Copywriter Romke Oortwijn **Agency Producer** Pieter van der Schaaf **Film Director** Othmar Sweers **Production Company** Czar Films

It's completed. The new BMW 3-series.

15 **TV & Cinema Advertising**   **Television Commercial**
National Award Silver **Title** The Gardener/Vacuum Cleaner/Freezer/Candyman/A Friend for Dinner **Agency** B.S.U.R. **Production Company** B.S.U.R. **Client** Foundation Weekend of Terror
Creative Director Joost Perik **Art Director** Rodger Beekman **Copywriters** Joost Perik, Theo Doyer **Agency Producer** Michael van den Heerik **Film Directors** Rodger Beekman, Theo Doyer

Weekend of Terror.

 16

 17

16 **TV & Cinema Advertising   Television Commercial**
National Award Silver **Title** John the Manager **Agency** Ammirati Puris Lintas **Client** Van den Bergh Nederland **Creative Directors** Diederick Koopal, Cor den Boer **Art Director** Cor den Boer
Copywriter Diederick Koopal **Agency Producer** Roosemarie Praaning **Film Director** Yani **Production Company** hazazaH

4 o'clock Cup a Soup, more people should do that.

17 **TV & Cinema Advertising   Television Commercial**
National Award Silver **Title** Goal! **Agency** Ammirati Puris Lintas **Client** Van den Bergh Nederland **Creative Directors** Diederick Koopal, Cor den Boer **Art Director** Ivar van der Zwan
Copywriter Jeroen Ragas **Film Director** Charlotte Kempers **Director of Photography** Hans Jonkers **Production Company** Jonkers Hofstee Film

How big do you want to be?

80% VAN ALLE ONGELUKKEN
GEBEURT ONDER HET TOEZIEND
OOG VAN OUDERS.

LEER SNELLER DAN JE KINDEREN.

BEL CONSUMENT EN VEILIGHEID
020-511 45 67

LAAT JE NIET VERRASSEN.

18

19

Het PAROOL

Beatrix Toff
leest Het Parool.
Abonnee sinds mei '84

Het PAROOL

Beatrix Pruijt
leest Het Parool.
Abonnee sinds januari '68

Het PAROOL

Beatrix van Puffelen Vos
leest Het Parool.
Abonnee sinds maart '91

Het PAROOL

Beatrix Lindveld
leest Het Parool.
Abonnee sinds oktober '88

18 **TV & Cinema Advertising   Public Service/Charity (TV)**
National Award Silver **Title** Funniest Home Videos **Agency** TBWA/Campaign Company **Client** Consument en Veiligheid (Child Safety Council) **Art Director** Ray Mendez
Copywriter Gregg Wasiak **Agency Producers** Miriam Buise, Ronald Milton

Don't be surprised by your child. Learn to prevent falling accidents.

19 **Posters   Poster Advertising**
National Award Silver **Title** Beatrix Reads Het Parool **Agency** KesselsKramer **Client** Het Parool **Creative Directors** Johan Kramer, Erik Kessels **Art Director** Erik Kessels
Copywriter Johan Kramer **Photographer** Gerdjan van der Lugt

20 **Posters   Poster Advertising**
National Award Silver **Title** Tear Jerker Festival **Agency** KesselsKramer **Client** Smartlappen Festival Utrecht **Creative Directors** Erik Kessels, Johan Kramer **Art Director** Erik Kessels
Copywriter Johan Kramer **Typographer** Anthony Burril **Photographer** Herman Pieterse

21 **Promotion**
National Award Silver **Title** Here Lies A Monuta Folder **Agency** Grey Advertising **Client** Monuta Funeral Service **Creative Directors** Erik Laging, Ron Lebbink **Art Director** Ron Lebbink
Copywriter Erik Laging

22

23

22 Promotion   Mailings
National Award Silver **Title** Nudists **Agency** linssen id **Client** Wosjh Italian Casual Clothing **Art Director** Maarten Bakker **Copywriter** Rob Linssen

Thank God the new summer collection has arrived.

23 Interactive Media   Distributed Media (CD ROMs, DVDs etc)
National Award Silver **Title** De Leeuw van Oranje **Agency** Direct Company **Client** Postbank **Art Directors** Nicole Cordia, Theo Imhoff **Copywriters** Hans van Dijk, Menno Schipper
HTML Operators Edo Schoonebeek, Bas Lenfert

The Lion of Orange.

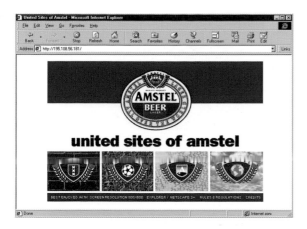

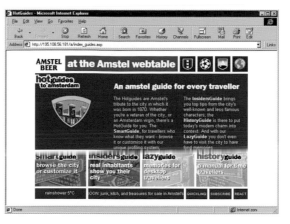

24

25

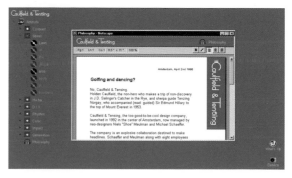

24 Interactive Media   Internet
National Award   Silver   Title United Sites of Amstel   **Agency** Ozz interactive   **Client** Heineken Brouwerijen Nederland   **Creative Director** Dagan Cohen   **Art Director** Dagan Cohen
Copywriters Dagan Cohen, Jules Marshall   **Designer** Caulfield & Tensing   **Photographer** Barbara van Ittersum

The Amstel site is the best source of information about the UEFA Champions League and offers the hottest and most attractive online guide for the city of Amsterdam.

25 Interactive Media   Internet
National Award Silver   **Title** Attitude Online   **Design Studio** Caulfield & Tensing   **Client** Caulfield & Tensing   **Creative Directors** Niels Meulman, Michael Schaeffer   **Art Directors** Niels Meulman,
Michael Schaeffer   **Copywriters** Niels Meulman, Michael Schaeffer, Adam Eeuwens   **Designers** Niels Meulman, Michael Schaeffer, Janneke Bergmans, Bas de Graaf, Geert Jan Mulder,
Christine van Rossum   **Photographers** Leendert Mulder, Maurice Scheltens   **Illustrators** Janneke Bergmans, TBHeadquarters

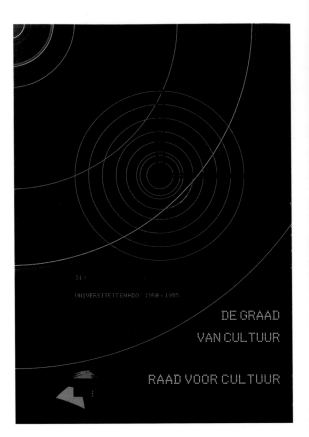

26

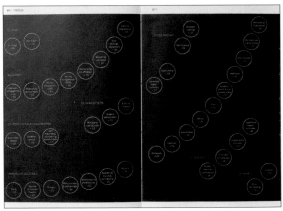

27

26 **Graphic Design   Corporate Identity**
National Award Silver **Title** Milk. Exams 1998 - Baseball/Kiss/Playstation/Breakdance **Agency** Schaeffer Wünsch Has **Client** Het Nederlands Zuivelbureau
Creative Directors Lode Schaeffer, Erik Wünsch **Art Directors** Will Holder, Maurice Scheltens **Copywriters** Will Holder, Maurice Scheltens **Typographer** Will Holder
Photographer Maurice Scheltens

Fast Forward. The white boost.

27 **Graphic Design   Annual Reports, Catalogues, Calendars, Compact Disks & Record Sleeves etc**
National Award Silver **Title** De Graad van Cultuur in 40 grafieken/Raad voor Cultuur jaarverslag 1997 **Design Studio** De Designpolitie **Client** Raad voor Cultuur
Art Directors Richard van der Laken, Pepijn Zurburg **Designers** Richard van der Laken, Pepijn Zurburg **Illustrator** Herman van Bostelen

Council for Culture. The level of culture in 40 figures. A new interpretation on the phenomenon "infographics".

28 **Packaging**
National Award Gold **Title** Care + Cure **Design Studio** Visser Bay Anders Toscani Design **Client** Bykare Nederland **Creative Director** Teun Anders **Art Director** Saskia Hellegers
Designer Saskia Hellegers **Illustrators** Tom Sohamp, Angeles Nicto, Femke Hiemstra, Simone Golob

29 **Packaging**
National Award Silver **Title** Albert Heijn Bath Foam & Shower Gel **Design Studio** Millford-Van den Berg Packaging Design **Client** Albert Heijn **Creative Director** Erik de Graaf
Designers Erik de Graaf, Ronald Lewerissa **Illustrator** Hans Reisinger

IRELAND

eire

1 **Nomination Illustration & Photography Illustration**
National Award Silver **Title** Irish Short Stories **Entrant** David Rooney **Client** The Polio Society **Art Director** Joe Whitlock - Blundell **Designer** Joe Whitlock - Blundell
Illustrator David Rooney

The new Volkswagen Polo Estate.

We had a little bit of trouble fitting the entire new Volkswagen Polo Estate into one ad. Luckily, lack of space is not a problem you're ever likely to encounter, as the stylish and economical Polo Estate is simply the biggest small car you can buy. And as you'd expect from a Volkswagen, it extends the small car far beyond its limits.

Volkswagen Polo. From £12,190.
For more information contact your local Volkswagen dealer. Delivery and related charges not included.

2

IBM

"oops"

The ultra thin IBM Flat Panel Monitor. With a stylish 16.1 inch screen, offering 16.7 million colours, it's   hard to miss. From the front. Call **0800 777777** or visit **www.ibm.com/europe**

3

2   **Print Advertising   Magazine Advertising**
    National Award Silver **Title** Beyond the Limits **Agency** Peter Owens DDB **Client** Motor Distributors Ltd. **Art Director** Donal O'Dea **Copywriter** Colin Murphy **Concept** Colin Murphy, Donal O'Dea **Typographer** Donal O'Dea

3   **Print Advertising   Magazine Advertising**
    National Award Silver **Title** Oops **Agency** Ogilvy + Mather Paris **Client** IBM Europe **Creative Director** A. Kuijvenhoven **Art Director** Tim Knox **Copywriter** Richard Ryan **Concept** Richard Ryan, Tim Knox **Marketing Manager** Josh Shapiro

★ 4

★ 5

4 **Print Advertising   Trade Advertising**
National Award Silver **Title** Fruit & Veg **Agency** Arks Advertising **Client** Heinz **Art Director** Carol Lambert **Copywriter** Dan O'Doherty **Designer** Carol Lambert **Photographer** Walter Pfeiffer
Concept Dan O'Doherty **Typographer** Carol Lambert **Account Director** Jimmy Murphy **Marketing Manager** John O'Reilly

5 **TV & Cinema Advertising   Television Commercial**
National Award Silver **Title** Remote Control **Agency** CDP Associates **Client** ESB **Creative Director** Philip Elliott **Art Director** Philip Elliott **Copywriter** Matt Dolan
Agency Producer Dave Brady **Film Director** Keith Hutchinson **Production Company** Halford Hutchinson **Lighting Camera** Tony Higgins **Editor** Tom O'Flaherty **Music** Amber

★ 6

★ 7

6 **TV & Cinema Advertising   Television Commercial**
National Award Silver **Title** Water/Wren Boys/Sky/Red Lemonade **Agency** O'Connor O'Sullivan **Client** TnaG **Art Director** Pat Hamill **Copywriter** Gavin O'Sullivan **Designer** Brian Williams
Agency Producer Pat Hamill **Producer** Justin McCarthy **Production Company** Dynamo **Concept** Pat Hamill, Gavin O'Sullivan **Lighting** Ciaran Tannam **Editor** Brian Williams

7 **Posters   Poster Advertising**
National Award Silver **Title** Slow Down **Agency** Irish International **Client** Aer Lingus **Art Director** Adrian Fitz-Simon **Copywriter** Des Kavanagh **Concept** Adrian Fitz-Simon, Des Kavanagh
Typographer Adrian Fitz-Simon

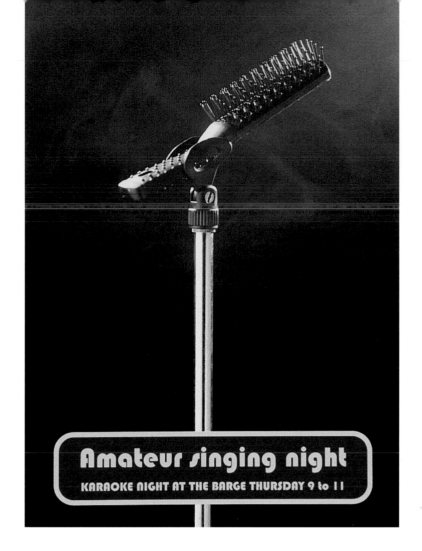

8 **Posters   Poster Advertising**
National Award Silver **Title** Hairbrush **Agency** McConnells **Client** The Barge **Account Director** Keith Murray **Marketing Manager** James Rice **Art Directors** Michael Walsh,
Fergus O'Hare **Copywriters** Michael Walsh, Fergus O'Hare **Photographer** Trevor Hart **Concept** Michael Walsh, Fergus O'Hare **Typographers** Michael Walsh, Fergus O'Hare

9 **Promotion   Mailings**
National Award Silver **Title** One for the Road **Entrant** Ian Doherty **Client** Saatchi & Saatchi **Art Director** Jo Clements **Photographer** Neil O'Reilly **Illustrator** Neil O'Reilly

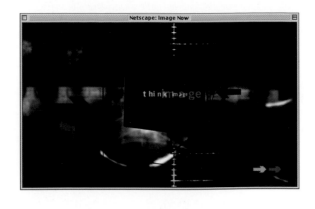

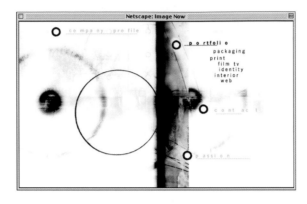

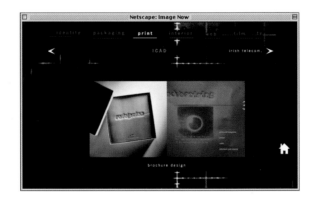

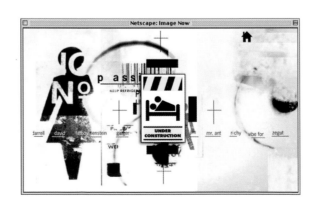

10 **Interactive Media** **Distributed Media (CD ROMs, DVDs etc)**
National Award Silver **Title** Website **Agency** Image Now **Client** Image Now **Art Director** Fabrice Robin **Copywriter** Malcolm Hamilton **Designer** Fabrice Robin

ITALY

italia

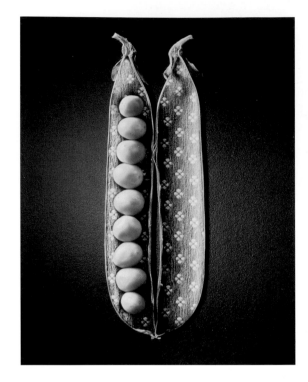

1 **Nomination** **Print Advertising** **Magazine Advertising**
National Award Gold **Title** Haas. Decorazioni d'interni dal 1811 **Agency** Leo Burnett Co. **Client** Haas Dal 1811 **Creative Director** Enrico Dorizza **Art Director** Rosemary Collini Bosso
Copywriter Luca Grelli **Photographer** Paul Bussel

Haas, interior decoration since 1811 - Pea pot/Carnivorous plant/Chest nut.

2 **Nomination   Illustration & Photography   Illustration**
National Award Silver **Title** La Pianta Grassa **Entrant** Marcella Peluffo **Client** Associazione Illustratori **Designer** Grafco **Illustrator** Marcella Peluffo

The Cactus.

3 **Nomination   Illustration & Photography   Illustration**
National Award Gold **Title** L' Incubo Del Sig Mario **Entrant** L' Incubo Del Sig Mario **Client** Associazione Illustratori **Illustrator** Marcella Peluffo

The Nightmare of Mr. Mario.

Entrare fuori, uscire dentro.

Ogni giovedi apriamo una porta. Per l'inferno e per il paradiso.

4 **Nomination   Illustration & Photography   Photography**
National Award Silver **Title** Inferno e Paradiso **Agency** Esseffe **Client** Avventimenti **Art Director** Fabio Ferri, Gianluca Pagliarulo **Copywriter** Stefano Maria Palombi
Photographer Pedro Meyer

Hell and Paradise.

5 **Nomination   Illustration & Photography   Photography**
National Award Gold **Title** Memoria **Agency** McCann Erickson Italiana Spa **Client** RAI - Radio Televisione Italiana **Creative Directors** Marco Carnevale, Paola Manfroni
Art Director Paola Manfroni **Copywriter** Marco Carnevale **Photographer** Marco Biondi

Memory.

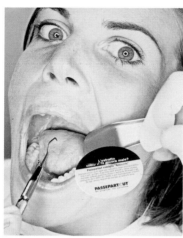

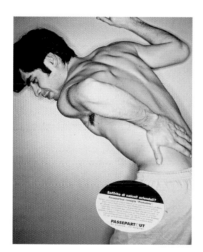

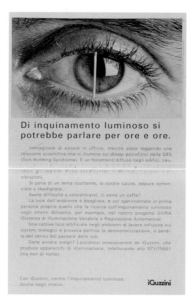

6

Di inquinamento luminoso si potrebbe parlare per ore e ore.

Come dovrebbe essere l'illuminazione nei nostri musei? Buona, buona, buona.

Compri un cashmere verde bottiglia, esci con un misto lana verde pisello.

Domanda: ritenete di essere più sensibili o meno sensibili di una zucca?

L'inquinamento luminoso ha fatto un'altra vittima.

Avete uccelli ridotti così, nel vostro giardino? Chiamateci.

---

7

6 **Print Advertising   Newspaper Advertising**
National Award Gold **Title** Malattie Aziendali **Agency** D'Adda, Lorenzini, Vigorelli **Client** Top Software **Creative Directors** Giampietro Vigorelli, Maurizio D'Adda
Art Director Giuseppe Mastromatteo **Copywriter** Joseph Menda **Photographers** Pierpaolo Ferrari, Davide Bodini

1) Are you afraid of financial dealings? 2) Withdrawing savings still a problem? 3) Suffering from company figures? (in Italian the word Calcoli means both figures or gall stones).

7 **Print Advertising   Newspaper Advertising**
National Award Silver **Title** Con iGuzzini Contro L'inquinamento Luminoso **Agency** STZ **Client** iGuzzini Illuminazione **Creative Director** Fritz Tschirren **Art Director** Fritz Tschirren
Copywriter Daniele Ravenna **Photographer** Jean - Pierre Maurer

1) We could go on for hours talking about light pollution. 2) What should lighting be like in our museums? Good, Good, Good. 3) You bought bottle-green cashmere, you got a pea-green wool blend. 4) Who do you think is more sensitive: You or a pumpkin? 5) Light pollution strikes again. 6) Should you be commiserating with the birds in your garden too? Give us a call.

8

8 **Print Advertising   Magazine Advertising**
National Award Silver **Title** Teleindipendenza **Agency** D'Adda,Lorenzini,Vigorelli **Client** Stream **Creative Directors** Giampietro Vigorelli, Maurizio D'Adda **Art Directors** Roberto Battaglia, Pino Rozzi **Copywriters** Pino Rozzi, Roberto Battaglia **Photographer** Roberto Micheli **Illustrator** Roberto Battaglia

1) We fight for those few souls (in Italian"four cats") who love theatre. 2) For some we're an interence (in Italian double meaning with nuisance) for you we're a signal. 3) There's a price to pay for independence. 4) Slavery is abolished. 5) Satisfy your taste for not being an audience (in Italian the word "audience" is used to indicate TV ratings i.e. number of viewers) 6) Pay per view has arrived. You choose what you want, you pay what you choose.

9 **Print Advertising   Trade Advertising**
National Award Silver **Title** Passata futuro **Agency** McCann Erickson **Client** Nestlé **Creative Director** Dario Neglia **Art Director** Matteo Civaschi **Copywriter** Francesca Pagliarini **Photographer** Luisa Valieri

Past (play on words: in Italian Passata could be interpreted as past) future.

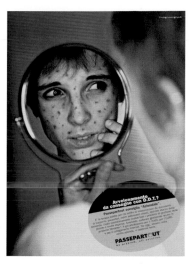

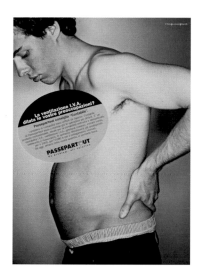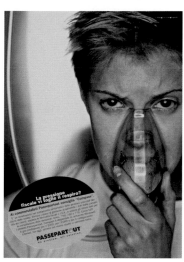

Visitateci.

10 **Print Advertising   Trade Advertising**
National Award Gold **Title** Malattie Aziendali **Agency** D'Adda, Lorenzini, Vigorelli **Client** Top Software **Creative Directors** Giampietro Vigorelli, Maurizio D'Adda
Art Director Giuseppe Mastromatteo **Copywriter** Joseph Menda **Photographers** Pierpaolo Ferrari, Davide Bodini

1) Delivery poisoning from D.D.T.? (D.D.T. in Italian means both D.D.T. (pesticide) and document di transporto 2) Does ventilating V.A.T. swell your worries? ("ventilation dell'IVA" is a system
through which the IVA tax is levied) 3) Financial pressures leaving you breathless.

11 **Print Advertising   Public Service/Charity (PA)**
National Award Gold **Title** Campanello **Agency** Saatchi & Saatchi **Client** Lega Tumori **Creative Directors** Stefano Maria Palombi, Luca Albanese **Art Director** Luca Albanese
Copywriter Francesco Taddeucci **Photographer** Valerio De Berardinis

POP IN : The cure for breast cancer exists. It's called prevention.

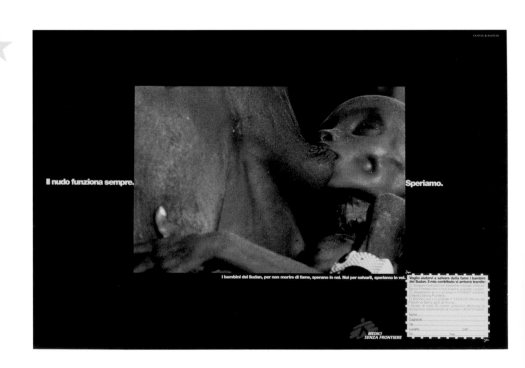

12 **Print Advertising   Public Service/Charity (PA)**
National Award Silver **Title** Boia Chi Lo Molla **Agency** McCann Erickson **Client** Lega Nazionale Difesa Del Cane **Creative Director** Milka Pogliani **Art Director** Paola Manfroni
Copywriter Stefano Campora **Designer** Paola Manfrin **Photographers** Image Bank, Immagine Zeta

Whoever unleashes him .... is an executioner.

13 **Print Advertising   Public Service/Charity (PA)**
National Award Silver **Title** Il Nudo Funziona Sempre.......Speriamo **Agency** Saatchi & Saatchi **Client** Medici Senza Frontiere **Creative Directors** Stefano Maria Palombi, Luca Albanese
Art Director Fabio Ferri **Copywriter** Stefano Maria Palombi **Photographers** Paul Lowe, Magnum, Contrasto

Nudity always works........we hope.

14 **TV & Cinema Advertising   Television Commercial**
National Award Gold **Title** New York New York **Agency** D'Adda, Lorenzini, Vigorelli **Client** BMW Italia **Creative Directors** Giampietro Vigorelli, Maurizio D'Adda
Art Director Giampietro Vigorelli **Copywriter** Maurizio D'Adda **Film Director** Federico Brugia **Director of Photography** Renato Alfarano **Title Music** Absurde **Music Composer** Fluke

New BMW 3 series saloon. Anything else is history.

15 **TV & Cinema Advertising   Television Commercial**
National Award Silver **Title** RAI - More of everything. Ballo/Amiche/Fidanzati **Agency** McCann Erickson Italiana **Client** RAI RadioTelevisione Italiana **Creative Directors** Paola Manfroni,
Marco Carnevale **Art Director** Claudia Chianese **Copywriter** Luca Miniero **Agency Producer** Fabio Cimino **Film Director** Simon Levene **Director of Photography** Sebastian Milaszewski
Production Company Cineteam **Scenographer** Marco Luppi

Non trovi le parole?

Cercale in un libro.

Il nudo in TV funziona sempre.

Il nudo in TV funziona sempre.

16 **TV & Cinema Advertising   Cinema Commercial**
National Award Silver **Title** Il Treno **Agency** McCann - Erickson **Client** Associazione Per il Libro **Creative Director** Antonio Maccario **Art Director** Roxanne Bianco
Copywriter Stefano Campora **Agency Producer** Riccardo Besso **Film Director** Brian Baderman **Production Company** BRW & Partners **Music Composer** Paolo Re

Can't find the words? Try looking for them in a book.

17 **TV & Cinema Advertising   Public Service/Charity (TV)**
National Award Gold **Title** Nudo **Agency** Saatchi & Saatchi **Client** Medici Senza Frontiere **Creative Directors** Stefano Maria Palombi, Luca Albanese **Art Director** Fabio Ferri
Copywriter Stefano Maria Palombi **Agency Producer** Fabrizio Conto **Production Company** Videocam/Cat Sound

Nude on TV always works. We hope.

18 **Posters   Poster Advertising**
National Award Silver **Title** PlayStation Party **Agency** TBWA Italia **Client** Sony Entertainment **Creative Directors** Enrico Chiarugi, Luciano Nardi **Art Director** Marco Gucciardi
Copywriter Enrico Chiarugi **Photographer** Lorenzo Scaccini

PlayStation party. Black tie required.

19 **Posters   Public Service/Charity (P)**
National Award Gold **Title** Campanello **Agency** Saatchi & Saatchi **Client** Lega Tumori **Creative Directors** Stefano Maria Palombi, Luca Albanese **Art Director** Luca Albanese
Copywriter Francesco Taddeucci **Photographer** Valerio De Berardinis

POP IN: The cure for breast cancer exists. It's called prevention.

20 **Posters   Public Service/Charity (P)**
National Award Silver **Title** Boia Chi Lo Molla **Agency** McCann Erickson Italiana **Client** Lega Nazionale Difesa Del Cane **Creative Director** Milka Pogliani **Art Director** Paola Manfroni
Copywriter Stefano Campora **Designer** Paola Manfrin **Photographer** Image Bank, Immagine Zeta

Whoever unleashes him ...... is an executioner.

21 **Promotion**
National Award Silver **Title** Invito Giuria **Agency** McCann Erickson Italiana **Client** ADCI **Creative Director** Alessandro Canale **Art Director** Sergio Marchino
Copywriter Alessandro Canale **Designer** Sergio Marchino

Samples.

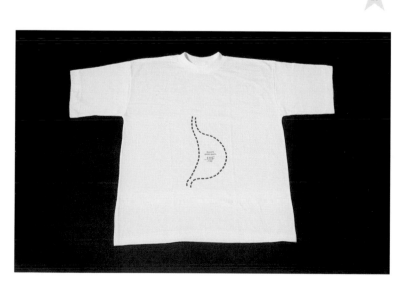 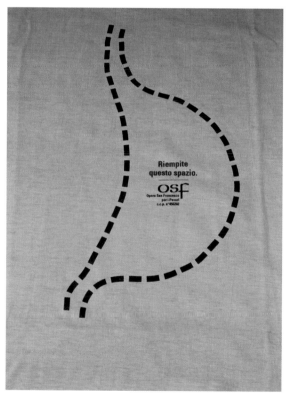

Riempite
questo spazio.

osf
Opera San Francesco
per i Poveri

22 **Promotion**
National Award Gold **Title** Testoni **Agency** Saatchi & Saatchi **Client** Federcalcio **Creative Directors** Stefano Maria Palombi, Luca Albanese **Art Director** Marco Palanca
Copywriter Francesco Taddeucci **Modelmaker** Gianpaolo Rabito

The earth is not endangered. It's the rest of the world that's endangered. Olympic stadium 16 December, hour 20.30. Italy versus the rest of the world.

23 **Promotion**
National Award Gold **Title** Stomach **Agency** TBWA Italia **Client** Opera San Francesco **Creative Directors** Enrico Chiarugi, Luciano Nardi **Art Director** Paolo Caspani
Copywriter Enrico Chiarugi

Fill in the space.

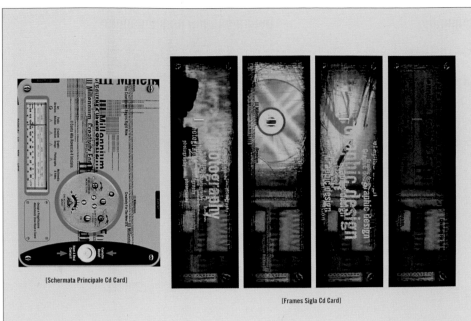

[Schermata Principale Cd Card]

[Frames Sigla Cd Card]

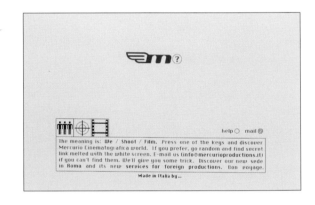

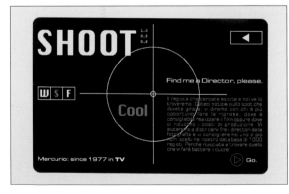

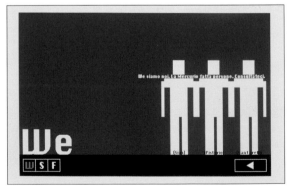

24 **Interactive Media   Distributed Media (CD ROMs, DVDs etc)**
National Award Silver **Title** Contatto Reale! **Entrant** III Millennium **Client** III Millennium **Creative Director** Elisabetta De Strobel **Art Directors** Federico Galvani, Giuliano Garonzi
Designers Federico Galvani, Giuliano Garonzi **Software Design** Sintetik Multimedia

The Millennium CD - ROM. Real Contact.

25 **Interactive Media   Internet**
National Award Gold **Title** Mercurio Cinematografica Internet CD - ROM **Agency** GNAF **Client** Mercurio Cinematografica **Creative Directors** Giorgio Natale, Federica Ariagno
Art Director Giorgio Natale **Copywriter** Federica Ariagno **Designers** Giorgio Natale, Federica Ariagno

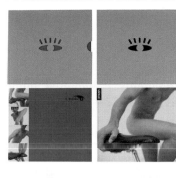

26

27

26 **Graphic Design   Corporate Identity**
National Award Gold **Title** The Invisible Gel Comfort **Agency** Bianchi & Kerrigan **Client** Selle Royal **Creative Director** Fabio Fedrigo **Art Director** Fabio Fedrigo **Copywriter** Corrado Castellani
Designers Piera Grandesso, Alex Miles **Photographers** Armin Linke, Alberto Narduzzi

27 **Graphic Design   Corporate Identity**
National Award Silver **Title** Caffé Nativo **Agency** Bianchi & Kerrigan **Client** Goppion Caffé **Creative Director** Fabio Fedrigo **Art Director** Fabio Fedrigo **Designer** Piera Grandesso

103 Italy

SPAIN

espana

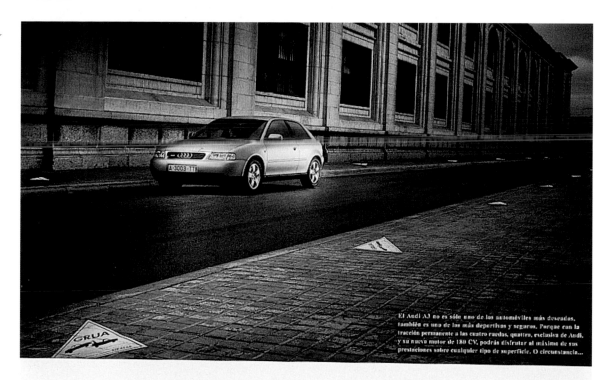

Nuevo Audi A3 quattro.
Nada se agarra más al mundo.

Audi ⊕⊕⊕⊕
A la vanguardia de la técnica

1   **Nomination   Print Advertising   Newspaper Advertising**
National Award Gold **Title** Tow Away **Agency** Tandem Campmany Guasch DDB, S.A. **Client** Audi **Creative Directors** J.L. Rois, A. Astorga, D. Ilario **Art Directors** D. Ilario, J. Badia
Copywriters A. Astorga, A. Binéfar

2   **Nomination   TV & Cinema Advertising   Television Commercial**
National Award Silver **Title** Harley Davidson **Agency** Tandem Campmany Guasch DDB, S.A. **Client** Audi **Creative Directors** J.L. Rois, A. Astorga, D. Ilario **Art Director** D. Ilario
Copywriter A. Astorga **Agency Producer** Vicky Moñino **Film Director** Pep Bosch **Production Company** Lee Films

3 **Nomination   Posters   Public Service/Charity (P)**
National Award Silver **Title** Blood **Agency** Young & Rubicam Madrid **Client** Red Cross **Creative Director** José Maria Pujol **Art Director** Francisco García Rodón
Copywriter José Maria Pujol **Photographer** David Levin

Donate your blood.

4 **Nomination   Packaging**
National Award Silver **Title** Pryca **Agency** Aguilera Morillas Ruiz, S.L. **Client** Centros Comerciales Pryca S.A. **Art Director** A.M.R. **Photographer** Jaume Malé
Illustrator María Alcobre **Design Director** Aguilera, Morillas, Ruiz, S.L.

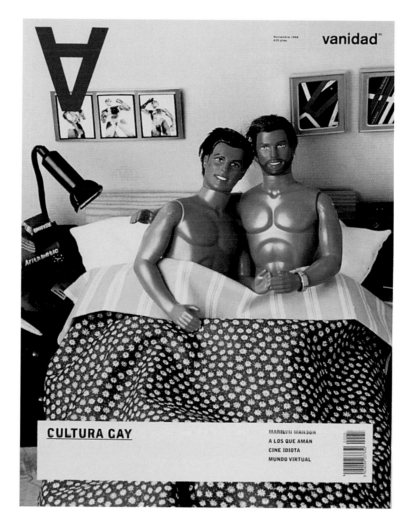

5 **Nomination Editorial**
National Award Gold **Title** Good News **Design Studio** Font i Prat Associats **Client** Actar Publishers **Creative Director** Ramon Prat **Art Director** Ramon Prat **Designer** Ramon Prat
Photographer Jordi Bernadó

The photographic work of Jordi Bernadó talks about the object and its context. The relationship between both of them is essential for understanding his work. How to show a work that talks about relationships with the context if in making the book we create another context more exterior such as the white that surrounds the image. This is not a book that contains reproductions of photographs, it wants to be a container of photographs. The paper support does not exist (only with the text). The touch of the cover reminds the albums of photographs.

6 **Nomination Editorial**
National Award Silver **Title** Drugs/Gay Culture/Liv Tyler **Design Studio** Grafica **Client** Egoiste Publications **Creative Director** Fernando Gutiérrez **Art Directors** Fernando Gutiérrez,
Mercia Fuoco **Designers** Xavi Roca, Salvador Huertas, Mercia Fuoco **Photographers** Johannes Wohnseifer, José Rodríguez, Dah Len

Vanidad - Vanity a new Spanish youth magazine about fashion/trends/music and film. Published monthly. The upside down A is a bulls head and relates to the A and V of Vanidad.

7 **Print Advertising   Newspaper Advertising**
National Award Silver **Title** Letraset **Agency** Vinizius Young & Rubicam **Client** Eddie Saeta **Creative Director** Joan Finger **Art Director** Jordi Almuni **Copywriter** Oscar Vidal

"Eddie Saeta." Love us or leave us.

8 **TV & Cinema Advertising   Television Commercial**
National Award Gold **Title** French Teacher **Agency** Tiempo/BBDO **Client** Planeta Agostini **Creative Director** José Gamo **Art Director** Javier Aristu **Copywriter** Nuria Argelich
Agency Producer Anna Morell **Film Director** Albert Saguer **Production Company** Rodar 2

Either you need a French teacher available all day long or you take the Planeta Agostini courses.

9 **TV & Cinema Advertising   Public Service/Charity (TV)**
National Award Silver **Title** Sangre **Agency** Young & Rubicam Madrid **Client** Red Cross **Creative Director** José María Pujol **Art Directors** Francisco García Rodón, Nuria Barahona
Copywriter José María Pujol **Agency Producer** Juan Isasi **Film Director** Xavier Roselló **Production Company** Errecerre

Donate your blood.

10 **TV & Cinema Advertising   Television Commercial**
National Award Silver **Title** Funeral **Agency** FCB/Tapsa **Client** Grupo Cruzcampo, Alvaro Rodríguez/Ada Bernal **Creative Director** Julián Zuazo **Art Director** Carlos Spottorno
Copywriter José Carnero **Agency Producers** Jesús Becedas, Marisa Rodríguez **Film Director** Bruce Stclair **Production Company** Lee Films

Life holds nothing worse and more terrible than the loss of a good friend.

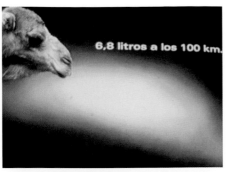

6,8 litros a los 100 km.

150 CV. V6

Honduras sigue necesitando ayuda.

11 **TV & Cinema Advertising   Television Commercial**
National Award Gold **Title** Kiss **Agency** Tandem Campmany Guasch DDB, S.A. **Client** Audi **Creative Directors** J.L. Rois, A. Astorga, D. Ilario **Art Director** D. Ilario **Copywriter** A. Astorga
Agency Producer Pedro Ramírez **Film Director** Tom Savin **Production Company** Monkey Films

12 **TV & Cinema Advertising   Public Service/Charity (TV)**
National Award Silver **Title** Mixer **Agency** FCB/Tapsa **Client** CODESPA Miguel Aranguren **Creative Director** Julián Zuazo **Art Director** Inaki Bendito **Copywriter** Miguel Bueno
Agency Producers Jesús Becedas, Javier Carrasco **Film Director** Igor Fioravanti **Production Company** Strange Fruit

Hurricane Mitch has wrecked the dreams of many families. This is a way of remembering what happened and making sure aid does not stop.

110 Spain

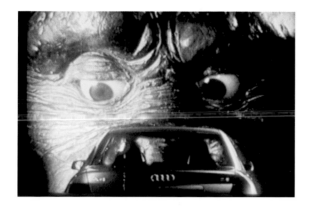

13 **TV & Cinema Advertising   Television Commercial**
National Award Gold **Title** King Kong **Agency** Tandem Campmany Guasch DDB, S.A. **Client** Audi **Creative Directors** J.L. Rois, A. Astorga, D. Ilario **Art Director** D. Ilario
Copywriter A. Astorga **Agency Producer** Pedro Ramírez **Film Director** Victor García **Production Company** Calle Cruzada

14 **TV & Cinema Advertising   Television Commercial**
National Award Gold **Title** EnglishTeacher **Agency** Tiempo/BBDO **Client** Planeta Agostini **Creative Director** José Gamo **Art Director** Javier Aristu **Copywriter** Nuria Argelich
Agency Producer Anna Morell **Film Director** Albert Saguer **Production Company** Rodar 2

Either you need an English teacher available all day long or you take the Planeta Agostini courses.

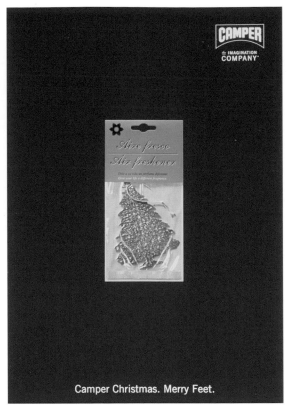

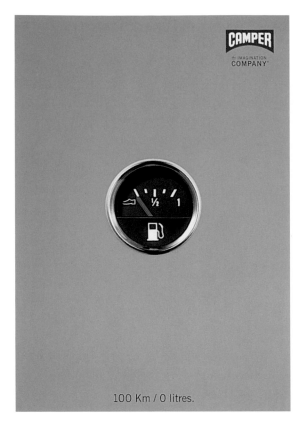

15 Posters   Poster Advertising
National Award Gold **Title** Camper Shoes Posters **Agency** David Ruíz + Marina Company **Client** Camper **Creative Director** Quico Vidal **Art Director** David Ruíz **Copywriter** Quico Vidal
Designers David Ruíz, Lisa Noble, Antón Molina **Photographer** Ramón Serrano **Design Studio** E.S.C. Comunicación

16 Posters   Public Service/Charity
National Award Silver **Title** Spring Festival **Entrant** L'Hospitalet Town Council **Client** L'Hospitalet Town Council **Designer** Peret

Poster which claims citizens attention on all the activities developed during this spring festival.

17 **Posters** **Poster Advertising**
National Award Gold **Title** The Tank Cultural Space **Entrant** Cristina Saavedra **Client** Cabildo de Tenerife **Creative Director** Cristina Saavedra **Art Director** Cristina Saavedra
Copywriter Cristina Saavedra **Designer** Cristina Saavedra **Photographers** Jaime Bravo, J. Carlos Batista, M. Angel Nalda

18 **Promotion** **Mailings**
National Award Silver **Title** Joke **Agency** El Callejón del Arte **Client** Grey Trace **Creative Directors** A. Vaquero, G. Silva, P. Torreblanca **Art Director** Menar Jiménez de Minana
Copywriter Susana Biedma

We were planning to kid around with you by leaving your car like this box. But we didn't know if you were a client of Fénix Directo.

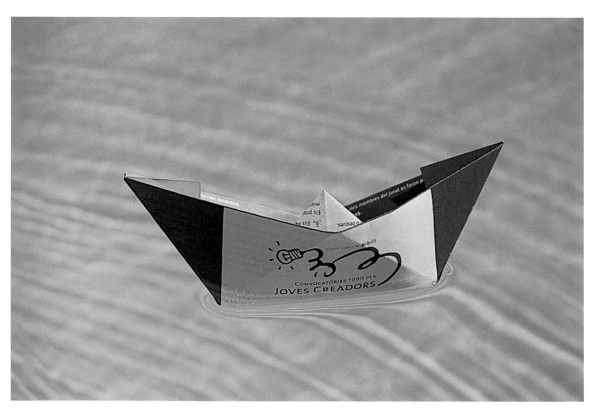

19 **Promotion**
National Award Silver **Title** +M **Agency** [bis] **Client** [bis] **Creative Directors** Alex Gifreu, Pere Alvaro, Martí Ferrer **Art Directors** Alex Gifreu, Pere Alvaro, Martí Ferrer **Copywriters** Alex Gifreu, Pere Alvaro, Martí Ferrer **Designer** Alex Gifreu, Pere Alvaro, Martí Ferrer **Photographer** Jordi Puig

20 **Promotion**
National Award Silver **Title** Masnou Young Creators Boat **Entrant** Marc Conca **Client** Masnou Council **Creative Director** Marc Conca **Art Director** Marc Conca **Designer** Marc Conca
Masnou Young Creator's boat.

21 **Interactive Media   Internet**
National Award Silver **Title** Escuchando imágenes **Entrant** Bernardo López Diaz - Rivavelarde **Client** Bernardo López Diaz - Rivavelarde **Creative Director** Bernardo López Diaz - Rivavelarde
Art Director Bernardo López Diaz - Rivavelarde **Copywriter** Bernardo López Diaz - Rivavelarde **Designer** Bernardo López Diaz - Rivavelarde **Photographer** Bernardo López Diaz - Rivavelarde

Escuchando imagenes is an exhibition of electronic images and sounds.

22 **Interactive Media   Internet**
National Award Silver **Title** Punto Blanco Banners campaign '99 **Design Studio** DoubleYou **Client** Industrias Valls 1 - Puntoblanco **Creative Director** Daniel Solana **Art Director** Blanca Piera
Copywriter Esther Pino **Programmer** Joakim Borgström

This web based campaign can be found at: http://www.puntoblanco.com/banner

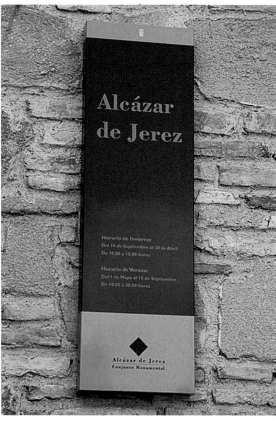

23 **Interactive Media   Distributed Media (CD ROMs, DVDs etc)**
National Award Gold **Title** Psicomanual Digital **Agency** MUBI Media, S.L. **Client** MUBI Media, S.L. **Creative Directors** Zush, Alex Net, Jordi Pernau, Xavier Colomer, J.M. Pinillo
Psicomanualdigitals Zush **Script** J.M. Pinillo **Co-ordinators** J.M. Pinillo, Alex Net **Infography** Jordi Pernau, Xavier Colomer, J.M. Pinillo **Programmers** Alex Net, Xavier Colomer
Setting up auxiliaries Dani Fernández, Pol Net **Music** Peter Gabriel, Zush -Tres **Music** Jumo **Sculptor Fuckface** Nico Nubiola **Typography Asura** Alex Gifreu
Packaging Albert Claret, Zush **Production** MUBI Media

24 **Graphic Design   Corporate Identity**
National Award Silver **Title** Señalización del Alcázar de Jerez **Design Studio** Gabinete de Imagen y Diseno del Ayuntamiento de Jerez **Client** Ayuntamiento de Jerez
Creative Director J. Carlos Carmona Otero **Designer** Juan Luis Munoz Trapero

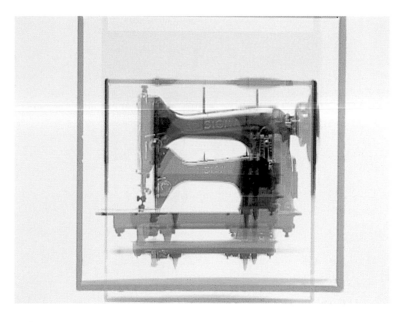

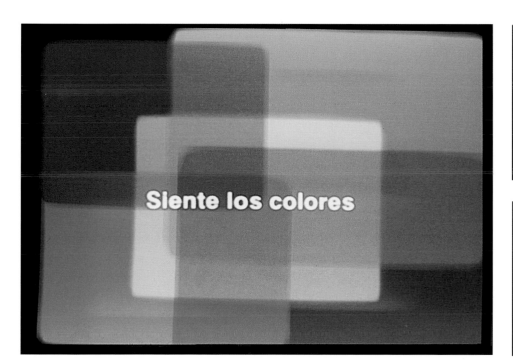

Siente los colores

25 **Graphic Design   TV Graphics (max 3 mins)**
National Award Silver **Title** Molinetes Sputnik **Agency** David Ruiz + Marina Company **Client** TV3/Canal 33 **Creative Director** David Ruiz **Art Director** David Ruiz **Designer** David Ruiz
Photographer Miguel Angel Nalda

26 **Graphic Design   TV Graphics (max 3 mins)**
National Award Silver **Title** Siente los Colores **Entrant** Autopromotion Dept., Taquilla, Canal Satélite Digital **Client** Canal Satélite Digital: Taquilla (PPV Channel)
Creative Director Jordi Bayo **Art Director** Pau Bosch **Copywriter** Jordi Bayo **Designer** Autopromotion Dept., Taquilla, Canal Satelite Digital

Feel the colours (Autopromotion for the football season 1998-99).

sverige

SWE
DEN

1 **Gold Award**   **Posters**   **Poster Advertising**
National Award Silver **Title** Voices from above **Agency** Lowe Brindfors **Client** NTF **Art Director** Mick Born **Copywriter** Olle Sjödén **Designer** Mick Born

There are two people that'll never forget me. My mom and the drunk guy that hit me.

2 **Nomination   Print Advertising   Newspaper Advertising**
National Award Silver **Title** Oxhagsroad/Lillångsroad/Sotarroad **Agency** TBWA Stockholm **Client** Telge Energi **Art Director** Patrik Sehlstedt **Copywriter** Anna Qvennerstedt
Designers Patrik Sehlstedt, Erik Bielke **Photographer** Sesse Lind

These ads were published in a local paper in a middle sized Swedish city. The pictures are of several different houses in that very town. (In total, there were 20 different ads with different houses.) People living in the houses did not know about the campaign until it appeared in the paper.

3   **Nomination   Print Advertising   Magazine Advertising**
    National Award Gold   **Title** Rain   **Agency** Hollingworth - Mehrotra   **Client** Pripps   **Art Director** Max Munck   **Copywriter** Hans Malm   **Photographer** Calle Stoltz

    Vichy Nouveau tastes better than water.

4   **Nomination   Print Advertising   Magazine Advertising**
    National Award Silver   **Title** The TV Screen   **Agency** TBWA Stockholm   **Client** MTV Europe   **Art Director** Henrik Delehag   **Copywriter** Anna Qvennerstedt   **Photographers** Sesse Lind,
    Johan Fowelin

5 **Nomination   Posters   Poster Advertising**
National Award Silver **Title** IKEA Malmö - Furnishing 1 **Agency** Forsman & Bodenfors **Client** IKEA Sweden **Art Director** Karin Jacobsson **Copywriter** Björn Engström
Decorators "Millan" Nilsson, Maria Zeilon

By furnishing poster sites, bus stops and other public areas in the city, IKEA celebrated the reopening of the IKEA store in Malmö.

6 **Nomination   Posters   Poster Advertising**
National Award Silver **Title** Lamps - Dull lighting/Day **Agency** Forsman & Bodenfors **Client** IKEA Sweden **Art Director** Anders Eklind **Copywriter** Filip Nilsson
Photographer Jäger Arén

This national campaign consisted of 10 different posters, each depicting an IKEA lamp and one see-through poster with the campaign tag line. These poster sites are all back lit making the lamps light up in the dark.

7   **Nomination**   **Posters**   **Poster Advertising**
National Award Silver **Title** Cage all kids **Agency** Forsman & Bodenfors **Client** Volvo Personbilar Sverige **Art Director** Mikko Timonen **Copywriter** Filip Nilsson
Photographer Magnus Mårding

8   **Nomination**   **Posters**   **Poster Advertising**
National Award Silver **Title** Local Newspaper III - Crooked **Agency** Forsman & Bodenfors **Client** Göteborgs - Posten **Art Directors** Staffan Forsman, Staffan Håkanson
Copywriters Björn Engström, Martin Ringqvist **Photographers** Photo Students, Vasa vux

9   **Print Advertising   Newspaper Advertising**
National Award Silver **Title** Forest Campaign **Agency** Romson **Client** The Swedish society for nature conservation **Art Director** Magnus Ingerstedt **Copywriter** Ola Gatby
Designer Mussi Rosander **Photographer** Carl Bengtsson **Account Director** Anna Kool **Account Manager** Paula Karlander

A pine can stay standing for seven hundred years.

10 **Print Advertising   Newspaper Advertising**
National Award Silver **Title** NK events 1998 **Agency** Romson **Client** NK Department store **Art Director** Anna Romson **Copywriter** Ola Gatby **Designer** Mussi Rosander
Photographers Pål Allan, Hans Gedda, Carl Bengtsson, Lasse Kärkkäinen **Account Director** Jan Lindforss **Account Manager** Anna Chantre

Today and tomorrow. Accessories days at NK.

Hör sångerskan
som nyss kom
hem från Afrika
där hon under
ett halvår levt på
endast kräftdjur,
insekter och
maskar.

Måndag 4 maj 12.00 i P2 presenterar Bengt Emil Johnson och
Stina Wohlström månadens P2-fågel: drillsnäppan.

SR Sveriges Radio

13

Far slår Mor. Lisa klär sin bror.

14

13 Print Advertising   Magazine Advertising
National Award Silver **Title** Treo Magazine **Agency** Garbergs Advertising Agency **Client** Pharmacia & Upjohn **Art Director** Petter Ödeen **Copywriter** Totte Stub
Illustrator Kerstin Pettersson **Final Art** Kerstin Pettersson

The campaign contained small advertisements for TREO pills for headache relief. Every advertisement is linked to a current event or the editorial material of the magazine. In a setting. Horoscope containing bad news for those born in certain signs. Just a little reminder for those born in Gemini.

14 Print Advertising   Magazine Advertising
National Award Silver **Title** Dad hits mum **Agency** Tennis anyone? **Client** Göteborgs Kyrkliga Stadsmission **Art Director** Fredrik Ganslandt **Copywriter** Daniel Röjnemark
Illustrator Carin Ax

Dad hits mum. Little one hits her brother.

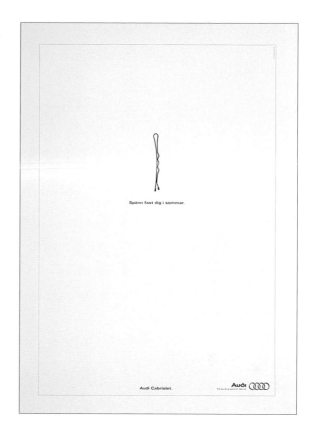

15 **Print Advertising   Magazine Advertising**
National Award Silver **Title** Fasten yourself, please **Agency** Stenström & Co **Client** Audi Sweden **Art Director** Hans Ahlgren **Copywriter** Greger Stenström **Photographer** Stefan Berg

16 **Print Advertising   Magazine Advertising**
National Award Gold **Title** Filmjölksskandalen **Agency** Paradiset DDB **Client** ARLA **Creative Director** Joakim Jonason **Art Directors** Joakim Jonason, Kjell Doktorow
Copywriter Jacob Nelson **Photographer** Mikael Engström **Account Director** Stefan Öström

Extra! Extra! All strawberries are gone. What will happen with the strawberry milk now, Arla wonders. The suspected Lord denies everything "sure, I like milk, but I know nothing about the strawberries". The ad in the right corner: Buy and enjoy before it's too late!

17 **TV & Cinema Advertising   Television Commercial**
National Award Gold **Title** Åke **Agency** Forsman & Bodenfors **Client** Svenska Spel **Copywriters** Martin Ringqvist, Jonas Enghage **Agency Producer** Maria Bergkvist
Film Directors Måns Herngren, Hannes Holm **Director of Photography** Mats Olofsson **Production Company** S/S Fladen

18 **TV & Cinema Advertising   Television Commercial**
National Award Gold **Title** Colonial Type/Parking Attendant/45 Minutes **Agency** Paradiset DDB **Client** Thomson Sweden **Creative Directors** Malin Carlsson, Björn Rietz
Art Director Malin Carlsson **Copywriter** Björn Rietz **Agency Producer** Anders Gernandt **Film Director** Jonas Frick **Director of Photography** Ivan Bird **Production Company** Modfilm
Account Director Helena Westin

19

VOLVO V70. FAMILJEBILEN.

20

Om du vill vara dig själv för en stund.

KLASS I

19 **TV & Cinema Advertising   Television Commercial**
National Award Silver **Title** Stray Dog **Agency** Forsman & Bodenfors **Client** Volvo Personbilar Sverige **Copywriters** Oscar Askelöf, Filip Nilsson **Agency Producer** Maria Bergkvist
Film Director Traktor **Director of Photography** Andrzej Sekula **Production Company** Traktor

20 **TV & Cinema Advertising   Television Commercial**
National Award Silver **Title** Class reunion **Agency** Paradiset DDB **Client** Spendrups Bryggerier **Creative Directors** Silla Öberg, Jacob Nelson **Art Director** Silla Öberg
Copywriter Jacob Nelson **Agency Producer** Anna Magnusson **Film Director** Traktor **Director of Photography** Traktor **Production Company** Traktor **Account Director** Stefan Öström

Nu med banansmak.

21 **Posters   Poster Advertising**
   National Award Silver **Title** We know the feeling **Agency** Paradiset DDB **Client** Thomson Sweden **Creative Directors** Björn Rietz, Malin Carlsson **Art Director** Malin Carlsson
   Copywriter Björn Rietz **Photographer** Erik Broms **Illustrator** Jeanette Andersson

22 **Posters   Poster Advertising**
   National Award Silver **Title** Monkey **Agency** Forsman & Bodenfors **Client** ARLA Milk **Art Director** Johan Eghammer **Copywriter** Fredrik Jansson **Photographer** Carl - Johan Paulin

   Now with banana flavour.

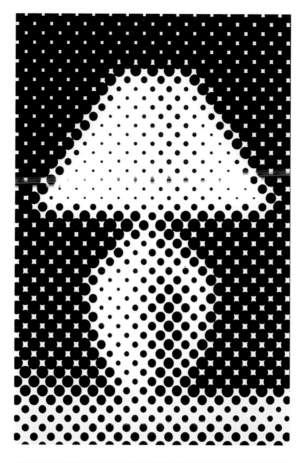

23 **Posters   Public Service/Charity**
National Award Gold **Title** Image Campaign Spring 98 **Agency** OCH Herrmann, Liljendahl & Co **Client** Vattenfall AB **Creative Director** Lars Liljendahl **Art Director** Lars Liljendahl
Copywriter Christer Alm **Designer** Kerstin Bernander **Illustrators** Björn Hedlund, Eduardo Espinosa **Photographer** Jan Bengtsson

24 **Promotion**
National Award Silver **Title** Notes **Agency** Forsman & Bodenfors **Client** Göteborgs - Posten **Art Directors** Staffan Forsman, Staffan Håkanson **Copywriters** Martin Ringqvist,
Björn Engström

These notes were posted all over the Gothenburg area in supermarkets, malls, and other places where notes like these might appear. For sale: Moped Yamaha DT 50. Look through the
"Motor" section instead. It can be bought at checkouts and has roughly half a million more readers than this note.

Varsågod! Den här plånboken är din.

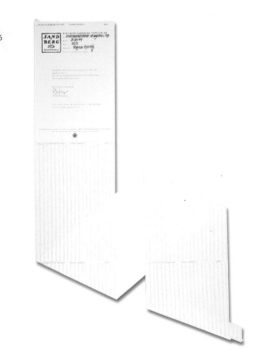

25 Promotion
National Award Silver **Title** Wallpaper by fax **Agency** BBDO.Allanson.Nilsson.Rififi. **Client** Sandbergs Tapeter **Art Director** Malin Köhlmark **Copywriter** Olof Gustafsson
Account Executives Ulrika Enghage, Annika Andreasson

Here you are, a sample from our new wallpaper – collection. This yellow wallpaper is called Hilda and is also available in several other colours. Best regards Staffon Sandberg.
P.S In a couple of days you will receive our new brochure in the mail. It's printed in four colours. DS.

26 Promotion
National Award Silver **Title** The Lost Wallet - A completely new media right out on the city streets **Agency** Fältman & Malmén **Client** Eurpeiska Travel Insurances **Art Director** Fredrik Claesson
Copywriter Bo Tidelius **Designer** Jarl Fernaeus **Account Executive** Fred Raaum

27

28

27 Promotion
National Award Silver **Title** The Red Cross Christmas fundraising **Agency** Hall & Cederquist/Y& R **Client** Swedish Red Cross **Creative Directors** Johan Öhlin, Claes Kjellström
Art Director Johan Öhlin **Copywriter** Claes Kjellström **Photographer** Carl Michael Björling

The Red Cross Christmas fundraising Account No 900800- 4. The aim of the campaign was to raise funds for the Swedish Red Cross and raise awareness of the organisation among people in Stockholm. At two of these squares, volunteers sold the small parcels (containing candlesticks in the shape of a cross) for the sole benefit of the Swedish Red Cross.

28 Promotion   Mailings
National Award Gold **Title** Swedish Stars **Agency** TBWA Stockholm **Client** BRIS **Art Director** Patrik Sehlstedt **Copywriter** Anna Qvennerstedt **Designers** Patrik Sehlstedt, Erik Bielke

These cards were given to all 12 year olds in Sweden from BRIS (children's helpline). The pictures are of Swedish famous people when they were young. On the back of each card is a story of that particular star and of his/her childhood difficulties. Every kid got 1 card and 1 letter from BRIS.

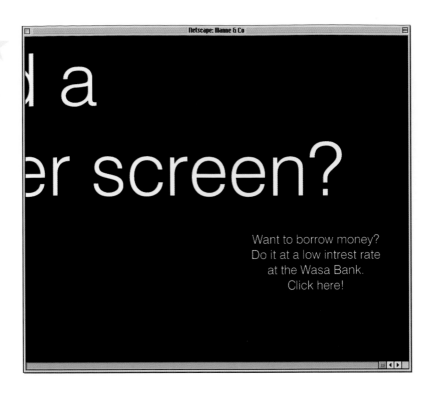

d a

er screen?

Want to borrow money?
Do it at a low intrest rate
at the Wasa Bank.
Click here!

29 **Interactive Media   Internet**
   National Award Silver **Title** Big Needs? **Agency** Manne & Co **Client** Wasa Banken **Art Director** Oskar Bård **Copywriter** Martin Stadhammar **Web Production** Speedway Digital Army
   Art Directors Assistant Kalle Haasum **Project Leader** Johan Larsson **Production Leader** Cilla Ardhall

   Need a bigger screen?

30 **Interactive Media   Internet**
   National Award Gold **Title** Your Private Web Shop **Agency** Romson **Client** Posten/Swedish Mail **Art Director** Magnus Ingerstedt **Copywriter** Ola Gatby **Designers** Anna Lilja,
   Nicke Bergström **Photographer** Martin Beskow **Design Group** Spiff industries **Account Directors** Jan Lindforss, Matias Palm-Jensen **Account Manager** Anna Chantre

31

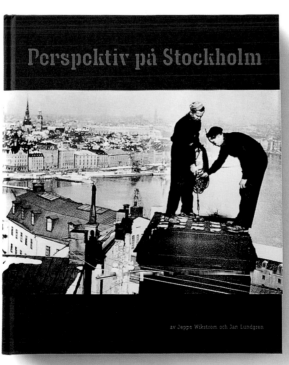

32

31 **Graphic Design   Corporate Identity**
National Award Silver **Title** Björn Borg Lanskapsdofter **Agency** Paradiset DDB **Client** Romella **Creative Director** Joakim Jonason **Art Director** Silla Öberg
Copywriter Birger Hedenheim **Designer** Silla Öberg **Photographer** Calle Stoltz

32 **Graphic Design   Corporate Identity**
National Award Silver **Title** Perspektiv På Stockholm/Stockholm Time and Again **Agency** Leo Form **Client** Bokförlaget Max Ström **Copywriter** Jan Lundgren **Designer** Patric Leo
Photographers Jeppe Wikström and others

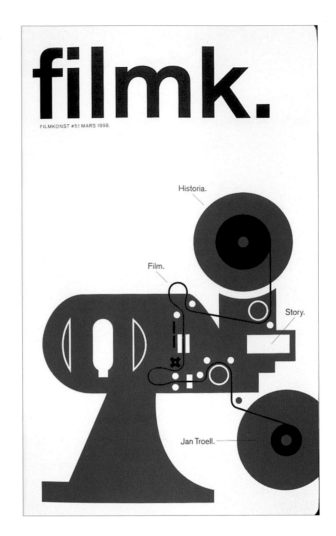

33

34

33 Graphic Design   Annual Reports, Catalogues, Calendars, Compact Disks & Record Sleeves etc
National Award Silver **Title** Filmk. **Design Studio** Greger Ulf Nilson AB **Client** Göteborgs Film Festival **Creative Director** Greger Ulf Nilson **Art Director** Greger Ulf Nilson
Copywriter Johan Croneman **Designer** Greger Ulf Nilson **Photographer** Jan Troell **Illustrator** ACNE

34 Graphic Design   Annual Reports, Catalogues, Calendars, Compact Disks & Record Sleeves etc
National Award Gold **Title** bob hund, "Jag rear ut min själ! Allt skall bort!!!!" **Design Studio** Firma Martin Kann **Client** Silence Records **Creative Director** Martin Kann
Art Director Martin Kann **Copywriter** Thomas Öberg, bob hund **Designer** Martin Kann **Photographer** Carl Johan Paulin **Illustrators** Roger Ericson, bob hund

My soul is for sale! Total clearance!!!

SWIT ZER LAND

switzerland

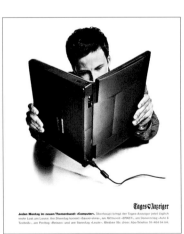

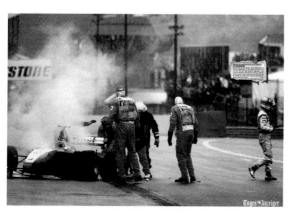

3 **Nomination** **Print Advertising** **Newspaper Advertising**
National Award Silver **Title** Tages-Anzeiger/Classified Ads **Agency** McCann-Erickson **Client** TA Media AG **Creative Director** Edi Andrist **Art Director** Daniel Comte
Copywriter Claude Catsky **Graphics** Roger Schreiber

4 **Nomination** **Print Advertising** **Magazine Advertising**
National Award Silver **Title** Quit smoking **Agency** Honegger/von Matt **Client** Quitsmoking Website **Creative Directors** Daniel Meier, David Honegger **Art Director** Daniel Meier
Copywriter Christoph Hess **Photographer** Staudinger & Franke

5 **Nomination   Print Advertising   Magazine Advertising**
National Award Silver **Title** Tages-Anzeiger/Classified Ads **Agency** McCann-Erickson **Client** TA Media AG **Creative Director** Edi Andrist **Art Director** Daniel Comte
Copywriter Claude Catsky **Graphics** Roger Schreiber

6 **Nomination   Print Advertising   Magazine Advertising**
National Award Silver **Title** Mobiliar Records **Agency** Publicis, Farner, Aebi, Strebel **Client** Die Mobiliar, Bern **Creative Director** Jean Etienne Aebi
Art Director René Sennhauser **Copywriter** Matthias Freuler **Photographer** Henrik Halvarsson

1) Cause of Damage (please describe circumstances). The fire damage to the building was probably caused by the careless throwing away of a passer-by. 2) Circumstances (please complete
if a police report was made). The telegraph-pole came towards me at high speed. I tried to swerve but the pole hit me right in the radiator. 3) How did the incident occur? I fell off the ladder
while installing a client.

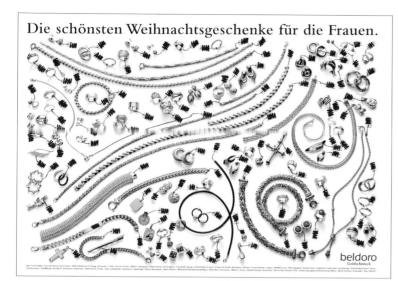

Die schönsten Weihnachtsgeschenke für die Frauen.

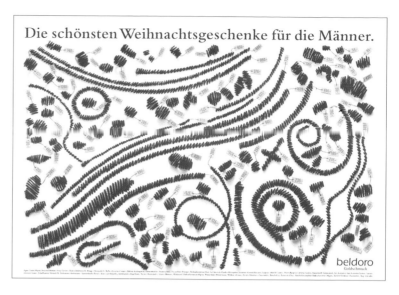

Die schönsten Weihnachtsgeschenke für die Männer.

Mit Hakle

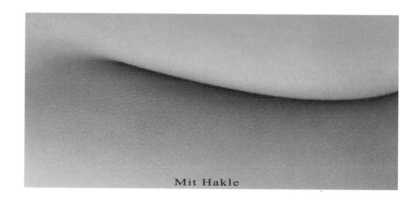

Ohne Hakle

7 **Nomination**   **Print Advertising**   **Magazine Advertising**
National Award Silver **Title** Beldoro Christmas Advertisement **Agency** Ruedi Wyler Werbung **Client** Beldoro AG **Creative Directors** Ruedi Wyler, Markus Ruf
Art Director Thomas Geissberger **Copywriter** Markus Ruf **Photographer** Alf Dietrich

1) All the most desirable Christmas gifts for women, 2) All the most desirable Christmas gifts for men.

8 **Nomination**   **Posters**   **Poster Advertising**
National Award Silver **Title** Smile **Agency** Advico Young & Rubicam **Client** Hakle Toilet Paper **Creative Director** Martin Spillmann **Art Director** Denis Schwarz **Copywriter** Martin Spillmann
Photographer Ronald Koetzer

WAS SIND
MEINE STÄRKEN,
MEINE
VORAUSSETZUNGEN?

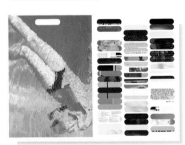

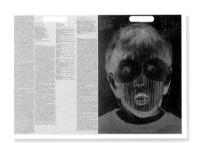

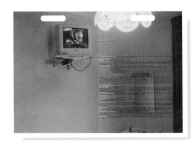

Art|30|Basel |16–21|6|99
The next international art fair

9 **Nomination   Editorial**
National Award Silver **Title** Company Report Migros **Design Studio** Studio Achermann **Client** Migros-Genossenschafts-Bund **Creative Director** Beda Achermann
Art Directors Markus Bucher, Andrea Muheim **Copywriter** Peter Ruch **Designer** Roger Furrer **Photographers** Daniel Sutter, Christian Kain, Annette Fischer, Thomas Flechtner
Illustrator Monique Baumann **Agency** ckdt. communications, Studio Achermann

10 **Nomination   Editorial**
National Award Silver **Title** Grenzwert Magazin Nr. 3 **Design Studio** Redaktion Grenzwert **Client** Bar Grenzwert **Creative Directors** Beat Müller, Wendelin Hess, Michael Birchmeier
Art Directors Beat Müller, Wendelin Hess, Michael Birchmeier **Copywriters** Max Küng, Michael Bahnerth, Michael Kathe

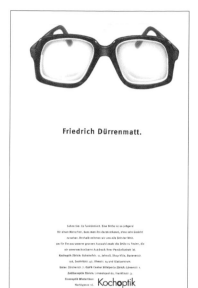

John Lennon.

Friedrich Dürrenmatt.

Kochoptik

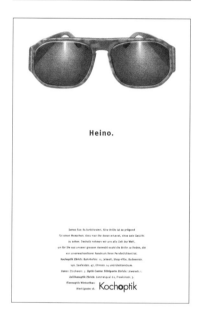

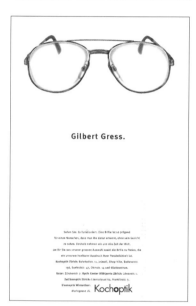

Heino.

Gilbert Gress.

Kochoptik

Kochoptik

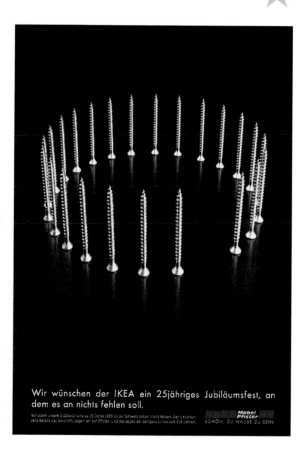

Wir wünschen der IKEA ein 25jähriges Jubiläumsfest, an dem es an nichts fehlen soll.

11 **Print Advertising   Newspaper Advertising**
National Award Silver **Title** Gratulationsanzeige **Agency** Lowe/GGK **Client** Möbel Pfister **Creative Director** Martin Denecke **Art Director** Philipp Sträuli **Copywriter** Mark Stahel
Photographer Tony Leimer

We congratulate IKEA on its 25th anniversary.

12 **Print Advertising   Newspaper Advertising**
National Award Silver **Title** Kochoptik Image Campaign **Agency** Lesch & Frei **Client** Kochoptik **Creative Director** Peter Lesch **Art Director** Olivier Marti **Copywriter** Thomas Lüber
Illustrator Bernhard Struchen

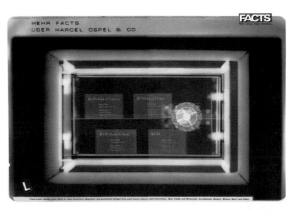

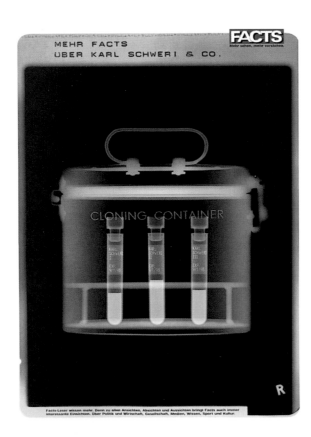

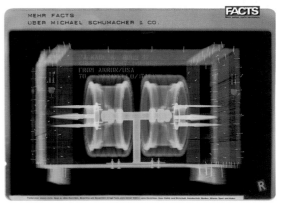

13 Print Advertising   Newspaper Advertising
National Award Gold **Title** Mobiliar "Records" **Agency** Publicis, Farner, Aebi, Strebel **Client** Die Mobiliar, Bern **Creative Director** Jean Etienne Aebi **Art Director** René Sennhauser
Copywriter Matthias Freuler **Photographer** Henrik Halvarsson

1) Cause of damage (please describe circumstances) The fire damage to the building was probably caused by the careless throwing away of a passer-by. 2) Circumstances (please complete even if a police report was made) The telegraph pole came towards me at high speed. I tried to swerve but the pole hit me right in the radiator. 3) How did the incident occur? I fell off the ladder while installing a client.

14 Print Advertising   Newspaper Advertising
National Award Silver **Title** Facts magazine **Agency** Publicis, Farner, Aebi, Strebel **Client** FACTS, Zürich **Creative Director** Jean Etienne Aebi **Art Director** Robert Wohlgemuth
Copywriter Matthias Freuler **Photographer** Chris Frazer-Smith

1) More facts about Karl Schweri & Co. 2) More facts about Marcel Ospel & Co. 3) More facts about Michael Schumacher & Co.

15 **Print Advertising   Newspaper Advertising**
National Award Silver **Title** Welcoming advertisement **Agency** Publicis, Farner, Aebi, Strebel **Client** Swisscom AG Mobile **Creative Director** Jean Etienne Aebi **Art Director** Luigi Del Medico
Copywriter Pascal Schaub **Photographer** Roger Schneider

Dear diAx, We wish you a successful launch into the mobile world. Yours swisscom mobile.

16 **Print Advertising   Newspaper Advertising**
National Award Silver **Title** Mobiliar "Turn" **Agency** Publicis, Farner, Aebi, Strebel **Client** Die Mobiliar, Bern **Creative Director** Jean Etienne Aebi **Art Director** René Sennhauser
Copywriter Matthias Freuler **Photographer** Nicolas Monkewitz

Even if nothing happens to you. You get money from us.

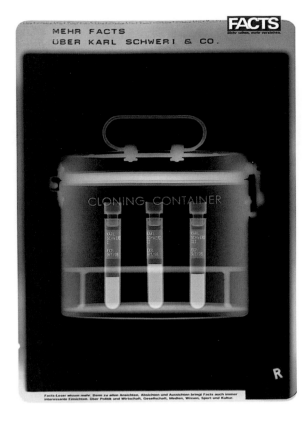

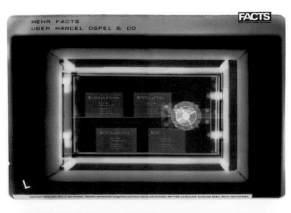

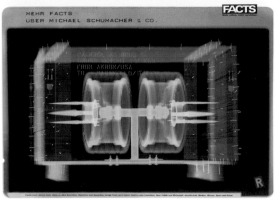

17

18

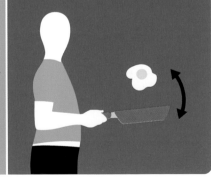

17 **Print Advertising   Magazine Advertising**
   National Award Silver **Title** Facts Image **Agency** Publicis, Farner, Aebi, Strebel **Client** FACTS, Zürich **Creative Director** Jean Etienne Aebi **Art Director** Robert Wohlgemuth
   Copywriter Matthias Freuler **Photographer** Chris Frazer-Smith

   1) More facts about Karl Schweri & Co. 2) More facts about Marcel Ospel & Co. 3) More facts about Michael Schumacher & Co.

18 **Print Advertising   Magazine Advertising**
   National Award Gold **Title** Vita Parcours Neulancierung **Agency** Weber, Hodel, Schmid, Werbeagentur AG **Client** Radix/Zürich **Creative Director** Reinhold Weber **Art Director** Uwe Schlupp
   Copywriter Beat Egger **Illustrator** Florin Wacker

   1) You'll find 12 more effective exercises for strength training at the new Vita Parcours. 2) You'll find 25 more effective exercises for mobility and agility training at the new Vita Parcours.
   3) You'll find 5 more effective exercises and great running tracks for endurance training at the new Vita Parcours.

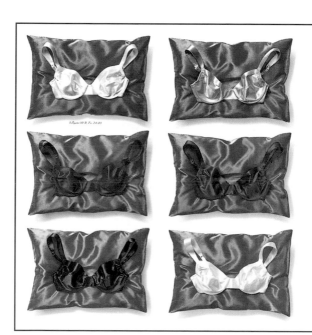

Bringen Sie doch etwas Farbe ins Büro.

Dieser BH ist einfach zu öffnen. Sogar für blonde Männer.

19 **Print Advertising   Magazine Advertising**
National Award Silver **Title** SSR Flight Campaign **Agency** Guye & Partner **Client** SSR Reisen **Creative Director** Danielle Lanz **Art Director** Danielle Lanz **Copywriter** Markus Ruf
Designer Dominique Oberwiler **Photographer** Patrick Rohner

1) Change of surroundings with wallpaper paste: from Fr. 3.95 per metre. Change of surroundings with SSR: from Fr. 0.000065 per metre. 2) Recommended holiday reading for anyone who wants to fly cheaper than with SSR. 3) Have you seen the three-hour commercial for our flights?

20 **Print Advertising   Magazine Advertising**
National Award Silver **Title** Triumph International **Agency** Wirz Werbeberatung **Client** Triumph International, Spiesshofer & Braun **Creative Director** André Benker
Art Director Barbara Strahm **Copywriter** André Benker, Hanspeter Schweizer **Photographer** Felix Streuli

1) Bring a little colour into the office. 2) As easily undone as the average man.

★ 21

★ 22

21 **Print Advertising   Trade Advertising**
National Award Silver **Title** Skybreaker **Agency** Guye & Partner **Client** SSR Reisen **Creative Directors** Danielle Lanz, Patrick Rychner **Art Director** Danielle Lanz **Copywriter** Markus Ruf
Designer Dominique Oberwiler **Photographer** Patrick Rohner

With Skybreaker you can save on the air ticket to extend your vacation. And with Eurotrain you can save on the rail ticket and stay even longer.

22 **Print Advertising   Trade Advertising**
National Award Silver **Title** Job Advertisement World Cup 1998 **Agency** Bozell Leutenegger Krüll **Client** Bozell Leutenegger Krüll **Creative Director** Mike Krüll **Art Director** Lukas Frei
Copywriter Antonio Lopez **Designer** Florian Stürzinger **Photographer** Oliver Nanzig

We still need three.

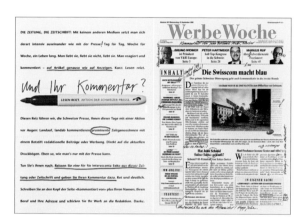

23 Print Advertising   Trade Advertising
National Award Silver **Title** Goodbye-Advertisement **Agency** Ruedi Wyler Werbung **Client** TA Media "DAS MAGAZIN" **Creative Director** Ruedi Wyler **Art Director** Thomas Geissberger
Copywriter Markus Ruf **Photographer** Nicolas Monkewitz

With this, we would like to bid goodbye to all our readers from the Berner Zeitung.

24 Print Advertising   Trade Advertising
National Award Silver **Title** Reading stimulates **Agency** Publicis, Farner, Aebi, Strebel **Client** Verband Schweizer Presse **Creative Director** Jean Etienne Aebi
Art Director René Sennhauser **Copywriter** Daniel Krieg

A swiss print media campaign. Newspapers, magazines: People's relationship with the print media is unparalleled; no other media type provides as much opportunity for intensive discussion as print media. And no other media type reacts and gives its opinions. In short: reading stimulates. In a two-week campaign, this stimulation was demonstrated to the public: All over Switzerland, dozens of prominent contemporaries commented editorial contributions with a red pen directly onto the printed sheet. A campaign possible only in printed media.

25 **Print Advertising   Trade Advertising**
National Award Silver **Title** Mailvan **Agency** Advico Young & Rubicam **Client** Mazda (S.A.) **Creative Director** Martin Spillmann **Art Director** Mathias Babst **Copywriter** Urs Schrepfer

26 **TV & Cinema Advertising   Television Commercial**
National Award Silver **Title** Job Interview **Agency** Advico Young & Rubicam **Client** Swissair **Creative Director** Martin Spillmann **Art Director** Martin Spillmann
Agency Producer Michela Trümpi **Film Director** Paul Meijer **Production Company** Planète Spots, Paris

27 TV & Cinema Advertising   Television Commercial
National Award Silver **Title** Wallwurz Box Champion **Production Company** Condor Films **Client** Stadelhofen-Apotheke (Pharmacy) **Creative Directors** André Benker, Jörg Birker
Art Director Jörg Birker **Copywriter** André Benker **Film Director** Michael Fueter **Director of Photography** Lukas Strebel **Agency** Benker/Birker **Music** Crazy Tunes
Sound Designer Peter Bräker

Wallwurz Ointment - wherever it hurts.

28 TV & Cinema Advertising   Television Commercial
National Award Gold **Title** Wrong Garage **Agency** Publicis, Farner, Aebi, Strebel **Client** Die Mobiliar, Bern **Creative Director** Jean Etienne Aebi **Art Director** René Sennhauser
Copywriter Matthias Freuler **Agency Producer** Karin Merk **Film Directors** Stefan Fraefel, Ernst Wirz **Cinematographer** Roland Schmid **Production Company** Wirz + Fraefel, Zürich

29 **TV & Cinema Advertising   Television Commercial**
National Award Silver **Title** Cash Image Spots **Agency** Lowe/GGK **Client** Cash Verlag **Creative Directors** Martin Denecke, Mark Stahel **Art Director** Willi Bühler
Copywriter Thomas Schöb **Film Director** Ernst Wirz **Director of Photography** Roland Schmid **Production Company** Wirz & Fraefel

30 **TV & Cinema Advertising   Television Commercial**
National Award Silver **Title** Schweizer Illustrierte VIP **Agency** Wirz Werbeberatung **Client** Ringier AG/Schweizer Illustrierte **Creative Director** André Benker **Art Director** Rolf Kälin
Copywriter Peter Rettinghausen **Agency Producer** Lilo Killer **Film Director** Michael Fueter **Director of Photography** Lukas Strebel **Production Company** Condor Films

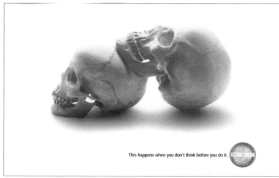

31 **TV & Cinema Advertising   Cinema Commercial**
National Award Silver **Title** Schweizer Illustrierte VIP **Agency** Wirz Werbeberatung **Client** Ringier AG/Schweizer Illustrierte **Creative Director** André Benker **Art Director** Rolf Kälin
Copywriter Peter Rettinghausen **Agency Producer** Lilo Killer **Film Director** Michael Fueter **Director of Photography** Lukas Strebel **Production Company** Condor Films

32 **Posters   Poster Advertising**
National Award Silver **Title** Think **Agency** McCann-Erickson **Client** Condomeria, Zürich **Creative Director** Frank Bodin **Art Director** Alvaro F. Maggini **Copywriter** Claude Catsky
Photographer Matthias Zuppiger, Andy Howald.

1) Think before you do it. 2) This is what happens when you don't think about it.

Dieses Plakat hat mehr Zuschauer als Night-Moor auf SF2. Wir bleiben dran.

Tages●Anzeiger

33

Viagra. Wir bleiben dran.

Streetparade: Der Tages-Anz-nz-nz-nz-nz-nz-nz-nz-nz-nz-nz-nz-nz-nz-nz-nz-nz-nz-nz-nz-nz-nz-nz-nz-nz-nz-nz-nz-nz-nz-nz-nz-nz-nz-nz-nz-nz-nz-nz-nz-nz-nz-nz-nz-nz-nz-nz-nz-nz-nz-nz-nz-nz-nz-nz-nz-nz-nz-nz-nz-nz-nz-nz-nz-nz-nz-nz-nz-nz-nz-nz-nz-nze-eiger bleibt dran.

34

Stündlich frisches Brot. Glatt.

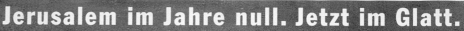

Jerusalem im Jahre null. Jetzt im Glatt.

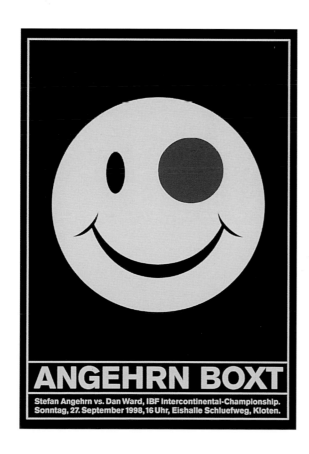

ANGEHRN BOXT
Stefan Angehrn vs. Dan Ward, IBF Intercontinental-Championship.
Sonntag, 27. September 1998, 16 Uhr, Eishalle Schluefweg, Kloten.

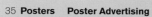

35 **Posters   Poster Advertising**
National Award Silver **Title** Glatt **Agency** Ruedi Wyler Werbung **Client** Glatt Shopping Centre **Creative Directors** Ruedi Wyler, Markus Ruf **Art Director** Thomas Geissberger
Copywriter Markus Ruf **Photographer** Nicolas Monkewitz

1) Fresh bread every hour. Glatt. 2) Jerusalem in the year 0. At the Glatt.

36 **Posters   Poster Advertising**
National Award Silver **Title** Angehrn is Boxing **Agency** Weber, Hodel, Schmid **Client** Stefan Angehrn **Art Director** Roland Hess **Copywriter** Tamás Kiss **Designer** Roland Hess

37 **Posters   Poster Advertising**
National Award Silver **Title** Flims. Laax. Falera. **Agency** Advico Young & Rubicam **Client** Mountain Marketing **Creative Director** Hansjörg Zürcher **Art Director** Dana Wirz
Copywriter Peter Brönnimann **Photographer** Julien Vonier

The Alpine Arena.

38 **Posters   Poster Advertising**
National Award Silver **Title** Bekenntnisse **Agency** McCann-Erickson **Client** Swiss National Railways (SBB) **Creative Director** Frank Bodin **Art Directors** Eva Keigel Markous,
Michael Schönhaus **Copywriter** Stefan Gigon

1) Charles Clerc: Where can First and Second Class passengers look far ahead without care? (NB: Play on words. First and Second Class may also refer to pupils in primary school.)
2) Andy Hug: Fill up on super, without gasoline? 3) Emel: Who gets young people off the streets? 4) Kurt Illi: Why can you go safely to any place in Switzerland? 5) Bettina Walch: For whom is
the weather not a topic of conversation?

39 **Posters   Public Service/Charity**
National Award Silver **Title** Romulus **Agency** Weber, Hodel, Schmid, Werbeagentur AG **Client** Schauspielhaus Zürich **Creative Director** Reinhold Weber **Art Director** Simone Fennel
Copywriter Tamás Kiss **Photographer** Stefan Minder

Romulus is a play written by Friedrich Dürrenmatt.

40 **Promotion**
National Award Silver **Title** Affront Schaufensterplakate **Agency** Weber, Hodel, Schmid, Werbeagentur **Client** Affront **Creative Director** Reinhold Weber **Art Director** Michael Rottmann
Copywriter Markus Rottmann

1) Pardon, Madam, but your blouse strikes us just like the white socks your companion is wearing. 2) Pardon, Madam, but we'd need four glasses of bubbly before braving the streets in that coat. 3) Pardon, Madam, how come your Pekinese looks more elegant than you do? 4) Pardon, Madam. that blouse you're wearing might be quite original in Ibiza. 5) Pardon, Madam, but your blouse has already come by here 25 times. 6) Pardon, Madam, but you'll never find a lover with that dress.

41 **Promotion**
    National Award Silver **Title** Remedies **Agency** Publicis, Farner, Aebi, Strebel **Client** Sportplausch Wider **Creative Director** Markus Gut **Art Director** Markus Gut **Copywriter** Matthias Freuler

42 **Promotion**
    National Award Silver **Title** SSR Travel **Agency** Guye & Partners **Client** SSR Reisen **Creative Directors** Danielle Lanz, Patrick Rychner **Art Director** Dominique Oberwiler
    Copywriter Markus Ruf **Designer** Katia Puccio **Photographer** Patrick Rohner

    With SSR travel you can save on the air ticket to extend your vacation.

43

44

Gewöhn deinen Magen schon mal
an amerikanische Portionen:
Zürich–San Francisco ab Fr. 925.–

SSR Reisen Buchungs-Telefonnummer 01-297 11 11

Wenn Chop Chop dich auf den
Geschmack gebracht hat,
bringt SSR dich nach Indonesien:
Zürich–Jakarta ab Fr. 790.–

SSR Reisen Buchungs-Telefon 01-297 11 11

Noch schärfere Thai-Küche als dieser
Take-away bringt nur ein Take-off:
Zürich–Bangkok bereits ab Fr. 720.–

SSR Reisen Buchungs-Telefonnummer 01-297 11 11

Schlitzohren geniessen die
chinesische Küche demnächst in China:
Zürich–Hong Kong ab Fr. 899.–

SSR Reisen Buchungs-Telefonnummer 01-297 11 11

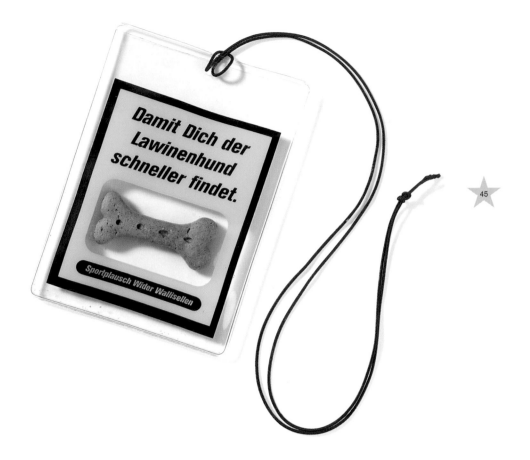

★ 45

★ 46

45 Promotion   Mailings
National Award Silver **Title** Snowboard Life Saver **Agency** Publicis, Farner, Aebi, Strebel **Client** Sportplausch Wider **Creative Director** Markus Gut **Art Director** Markus Gut
Copywriter Matthias Freuler

So the avalanche search dog will find you sooner.

46 Promotion   Mailings
National Award Silver **Title** Door Hanger **Agency** Guye & Partner **Client** Podere Il Casale **Creative Director** Danielle Lanz **Art Director** Priska Meyer **Copywriter** Markus Ruf
Designer Katja Puccio **Illustrator** Hannes Binder

1) Fitness Facilities. A full range of keep-fit facilities for our holiday guests. Picking olives to stretch your back, treading grapes to build up the calf muscles etc. 2) Order for breakfast. A parody of the way breakfast is usually ordered at luxury hotels. Except on this alternative style farm you can choose eggs you want to eat (Alberta, Gisela...), the cow whose milk you want to drink (Bruna...) and the poor pig whose bacon you want to eat. 3) Please make up the room yourself. 4) Entertainment programme. 10:00 Silence of the Lambs. After a heavy breakfast you take the sheep out into the meadow. It's incredible how quiet and trusting they are. Almost as if they had no idea that lamb was on the menu for tomorrow.

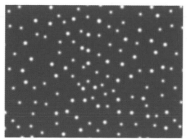

47

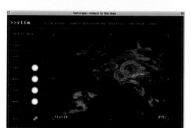 49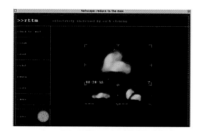

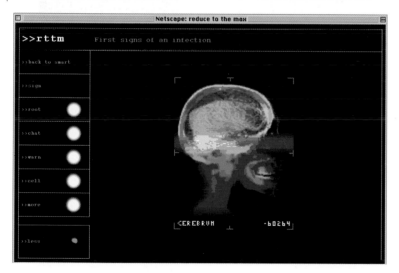

48

47 **Promotion   Mailings**
National Award Silver **Title** Leise rieselt der Schnee **Agency** Bozell Leutenegger Krüll **Client** Bozell Leutenegger Krüll **Creative Director** Mike Krüll **Art Director** Heinz Schwegler
Copywriter Mike Krüll **Designer/Production** Selmi Tonstudio

Christmas Greeting Tape "THE SNOW QUIETLY FALLS". Explanation: On television, when the television programme is disturbed, you can see something like a snowfall. In German this is called TV Snow. The video picture is blank, just showing TV snow, but you can hear singers singing the German Christmas song "Leise rieselt der Schnee" (The snow quietly falls). The singers are invisible because of the heavy TV-snowfall.

48 **Interactive Media   Internet**
National Award Gold **Title** Goodbye world! **Agency** R.Ø.S.A Internet and Conception **Client** R.Ø.S.A Internet and Conception **Creative Directors** Marcy Burt Butz, Sarah Burt
Illustrator Sarah Burt **Text** Marcy Burt Butz, Sarah Burt **Screen Design** Sarah Burt, Marcy Burt Butz **Coding** Sarah Burt, Marcy Burt Butz, Daniel Udatny

www.goodbye-world.com

49 **Interactive Media   Internet**
National Award Silver **Title** Reduce to the max - rttm_virus **Agency** R.Ø.S.A Internet Concept and Creation **Client** Micro Compact Car AG/W.H.S. Smart Communications Factory
Managing Director Bettina Korn **Product Manager** H.J. Schär **Creative Director** Marcy Burt Butz **Art Director** Patrick Spahr **Text** Marcy Burt Butz **Illustrator** Patrick Spahr
Concept R.Ø.S.A. Team **Clients Consultants** Marcy Burt Butz, Daniel Udatny **Screen Design** Marcy Burt Butz, Patrick Spahr **Coding** Daniel Udatny, Moritz Zimmer

rttm.smart.com/index2.html

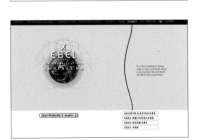

50

51

52

50 **Interactive Media   Internet**
National Award Silver **Title** www.ebel.ch **Agency** Headbanger **Client** Ebel, SA **Creative Directors** Alex Baillod, Pierre Rebetez **Directors** Alex Baillod, Pierre Rebetez **Designer** Amin Ladhani
Code Design Laurent Zimmerli

51 **Graphic Design   Corporate Identity**
National Award Silver **Title** The Wetzer **Agency** Galbucci Werbeagentur AG **Client** Wetzer GMBH **Art Director** Manuel Helwich **Copywriter** Alexandre Michael Hoster
Photographer Patrick Rohner **Illustrator** Max Grüter

52 **Graphic Design   Corporate Identity**
National Award Silver **Title** PODERE IL CASALE CI **Agency** Guye & Partner **Client** PODERE IL CASALE **Creative Director** Danielle Lanz **Art Director** Priska Meyer **Designer** Katia Puccio
Illustrator Hannes Binder

162 Switzerland

united kingdom

UK

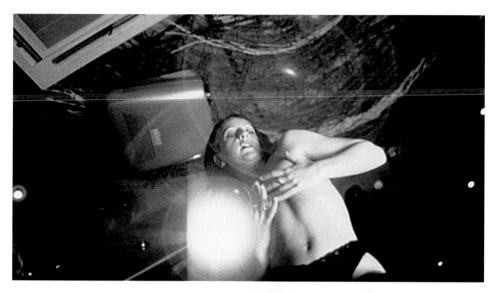

1 **Grand Prix Award**   **TV & Cinema Advertising**   **Cinema Commercial**
National Award Silver **Title** Litany **Agency** Lowe Howard-Spink **Client** The Independent Newspaper **Creative Director** Paul Weinberger **Art Director** Charles Inge
Copywriter Charles Inge **Agency Producer** Charles Crisp **Director** Rob Sanders **Production Company** HLA **Editor** Tim Fulford **Lighting Camera** Bob Pendar - Hughes
Music Composers Joe Campbell, Paul Hart **Producer** Helen Langridge

Life's pleasures are often frowned upon: this list of don'ts ("Don't fry your food, do drugs, breathe...") alludes to the free spirit of the paper's readers.

2 **Gold Award**   **Print Advertising**   **Newspaper Advertising**
National Award Silver **Title** Wedding **Agency** BMP DDB **Client** Volkswagen **Creative Director** Jeremy Craigen **Art Director** Neil Dawson **Copywriter** Clive Pickering
Photographer Paul Reas **Typographer** FGDS

 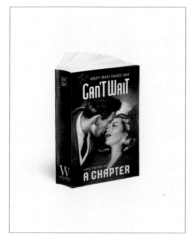 

  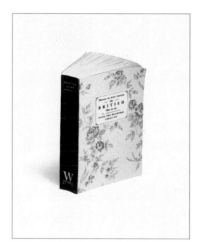

3 **Gold Award** **Print Advertising** **Magazine Advertising**
National Award Silver **Title** Quiet Child/Can't Wait/Coffee/Clairvoyant/Mistakes/Bedroom Light **Agency** TBWA **Client** Waterstone's Booksellers **Creative Director** Trevor Beattie
Art Director Paul Belford **Copywriter** Nigel Roberts **Photographer** Laurie Haskell **Illustrators** Mick Brownfield, Paul Belford, J. Otto Seibold **Typographers** Paul Belford,
J. Otto Seibold, Alan Dempsey, Nigel Ward, Alison Wills

167 UK

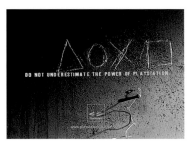

4   **Gold Award   TV & Cinema Advertising   Television Commercial**
National Award Silver **Title** Double Life **Agency** TBWA **Client** Sony Computer Entertainment **Creative Director** Trevor Beattie **Art Director** Ed Morris **Copywriter** James Sinclair
Agency Producer Dianne Croll **Director** Frank Budgen **Production Company** Gorgeous **Producer** Paul Rothwell **Editor** John Smith **Lighting Camera** Frank Budgen
Music Composer Fauré **Sound Designer** Hass I Iassan

Ordinary people become night-time warriors (not just people with no social life) maiming and generally leading a life of exhilaration… thanks to PlayStation.

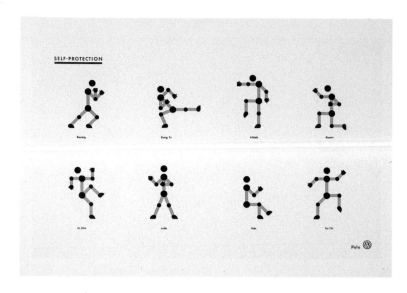

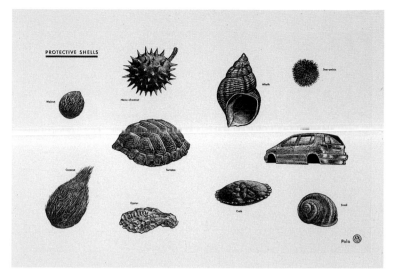

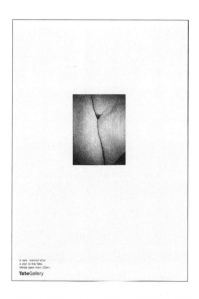

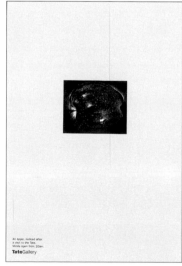

5 **Nomination   Print Advertising   Newspaper Advertising**
National Award Silver **Title** Fighters/Shells **Agency** BMP DDB **Client** Volkswagen **Creative Directors** Dave Dye, Sean Doyle **Art Director** Dave Dye **Copywriter** Sean Doyle
Illustrators Christopher Wormell, Jeff Fisher, Tilly Northedge **Typographer** David Wakefield

6 **Nomination   Print Advertising   Newspaper Advertising**
National Award Silver **Title** Rock/Conker/Apple/Vine **Agency** TBWA **Client** The Tate Gallery **Creative Director** Trevor Beattie **Art Director** Paul Belford **Copywriter** Nigel Roberts
Photographers Bruno Munari, Tessa Traeger, Peter Knapp, Michael Liam Cimiskey, Andreas Heumann **Typographer** Paul Belford

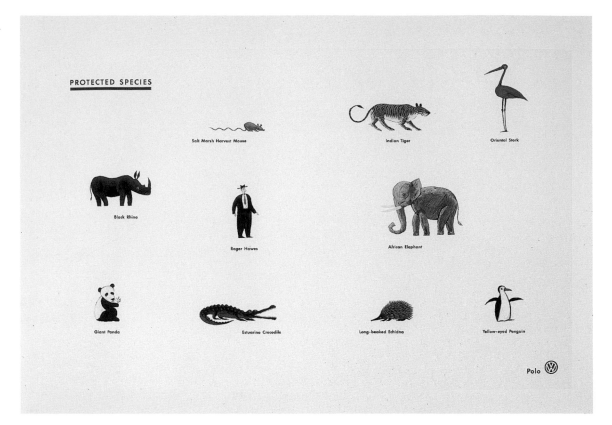

7 **Nomination   Print Advertising   Magazine Advertising**
National Award Silver **Title** Fighters/Shells/Species **Agency** BMP DDB **Client** Volkswagen **Creative Directors** Dave Dye, Sean Doyle **Art Director** Dave Dye **Copywriter** Sean Doyle
Illustrators Christopher Wormell, Jeff Fisher, Tilly Northedge **Typographer** David Wakefield

8 **Nomination   TV & Cinema Advertising   Television Commercial**
National Award Silver **Title** Swimblack **Agency** Abbott Mead Vickers - BBDO **Client** Guinness **Creative Director** David Abbott **Art Director** Walter Campbell **Copywriter** Tom Carty
Agency Producer Yvonne Chalkley **Director** Jonathan Glazer **Production Company** Academy **Producer** Nick Morris **Editor** Rick Lawley **Lighting Camera** Ivan Bird
Music Composer/Arranger Perez Prado **Sound Designer** Tony Rapaccioli

60 year-old Olympic local hero completes swimming course in the time it takes to pour a pint of Guinness - with a little help from his brother.

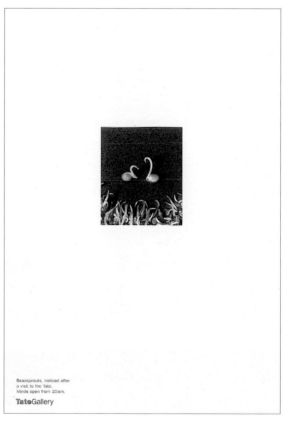

A piece of wood, noticed
after a visit to the Tate.
Minds open from 10am.

TateGallery

Beansprouts, noticed after
a visit to the Tate.
Minds open from 10am.

TateGallery

9   **Nomination   Posters   Poster Advertising**
National Award Silver **Title** Coffee **Agency** TBWA **Client** Waterstone's Booksellers **Creative Director** Trevor Beattie **Art Director** Paul Belford **Copywriter** Nigel Roberts
Photographer Laurie Haskell **Illustrators** Mick Brownfield, Paul Belford, J. Otto Seibold **Typographers** Paul Belford, J. Otto Seibold, Alan Dempsey, Nigel Ward, Alison Wills

10 **Nomination   Posters   Poster Advertising**
National Award Silver **Title** Wood/Beansprouts **Agency** TBWA **Client** The Tate Gallery **Creative Director** Trevor Beattie **Art Director** Paul Belford **Copywriter** Nigel Roberts
Photographers Bruno Munari, Tessa Traeger, Peter Knapp, Paul Caponigro, Michael Liam Cimiskey, Andreas Heumann **Typographer** Paul Belford

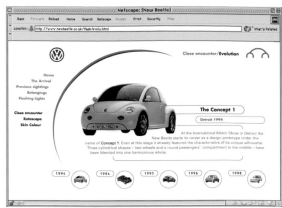

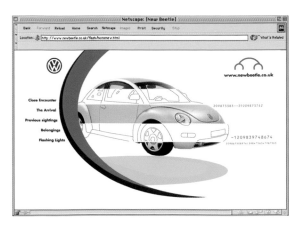

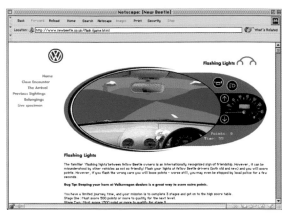

11 **Nomination   Interactive Media   Internet**
 National Award Silver **Title** New Beetle Website **Design Studio** Deepend Design **Client** Carat Interactive, Volkswagen UK **Creative Design/Directors** David Streek, Fred Flade
 Interactive Designers Pete Everett, Fred Flade **Graphic Designer** Fred Flade **Programmers** Gabriel Bucknall, Pete Everett **Copywriter** Ralph Pearce **Photographer** Panomania
 Music Composers Fred Flade, Pete Everett **Production Company** Deepend

 www.newbeetle.co.uk

12 **Nomination   Graphic Design   Annual Reports, Catalogues, Calendars, Compact Disks & Record Sleeves etc**
 National Award Silver **Title** One Woman's Wardrobe **Design Studio** Area **Client** Jill Ritblat/Violette Editions **Creative Director** Richard Smith **Designers** Richard Smith, John Dowling
 Design Directors Richard Smith, Cara Gallardo **Photographer** Toby McFarlan Pond **Typographers** Richard Smith, John Dowling **Editor** Robert Violette **Publisher** Violette Editions

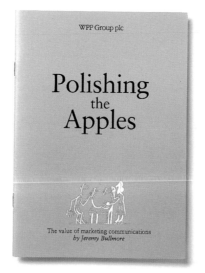

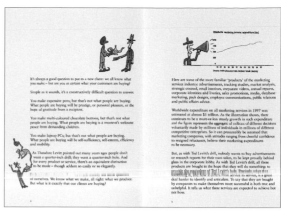

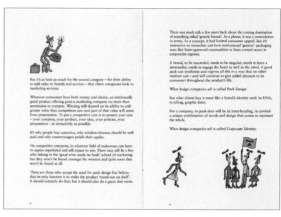

13

14

13 **Nomination** **Editorial**
National Award Silver **Title** Polishing the Apples **Design Studio** Addison Design Company **Client** WPP Group plc **Design Director** Peter Chodel **Copywriter** Jeremy Bullmore
Designer Tammy Kustow **Typographer** Tammy Kustow **Illustrator** Benoît Jacques

14 **Nomination** **Editorial**
National Award Silver **Title** The Pocket Canons: Words of the Wise **Design Studio** Pentagram Design **Client** Canongate Books **Design Director** Angus Hyland **Designer** Angus Hyland

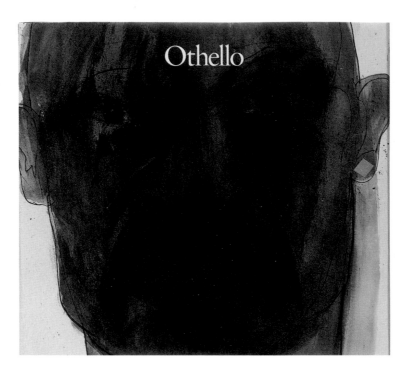

Othello

NO EVIDENC
OF NOSTALGI

15 **Nomination** **Editorial**
National Award Silver **Title** Shakespeare's Othello **Design Studio** The Chase Creative Consultants **Client** Alibaba Verlag **Design Director** Ben Casey **Illustrator** David Hughes
Designers David Hughes, Ben Casey, Tommy Shaughnessy **Copywriter** David Hughes **Typographer** Tommy Shaughnessy

16 **Nomination** **Editorial**
National Award Silver **Title** One Woman's Wardrobe **Design Studio** Area **Client** Jill Ritblat/Violette Editions **Creative Director** Richard Smith **Designers** Richard Smith, John Dowling
Design Directors Richard Smith, Cara Gallardo **Photographer** Toby McFarlan Pond **Typographers** Richard Smith, John Dowling **Editor** Robert Violette **Publisher** Violette Editions

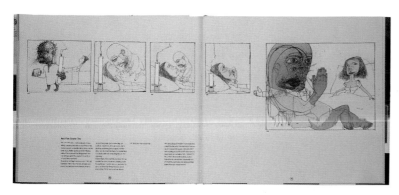

17 Nomination   Illustration & Photography   Illustration
National Award Silver **Title** Shakespeare's Othello **Design Studio** The Chase Creative Consultants **Client** Alibaba Verlag **Design Director** Ben Casey **Illustrator** David Hughes
Designers David Hughes, Ben Casey, Tommy Shaughnessy **Copywriter** David Hughes **Typographer** Tommy Shaughnessy

18 Nomination   Illustration & Photography   Photography
National Award Silver **Title** The Pocket Canons: Words of the Wise **Design Studio** Pentagram Design **Client** Canongate Books **Design Director** Angus Hyland **Designer** Angus Hyland

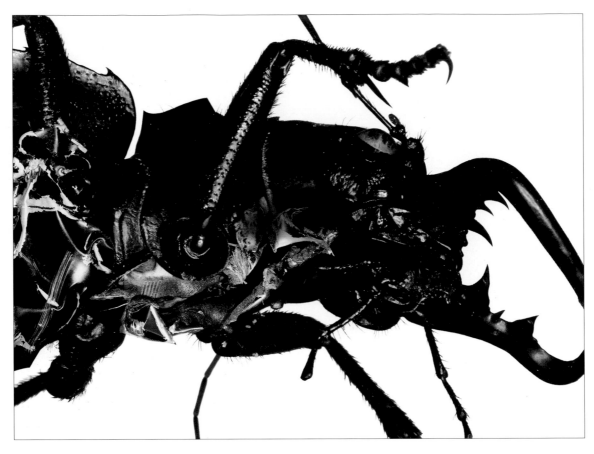

19 **Nomination   Illustration & Photography   Photography**
National Award Silver **Title** Massive Attack - Mezzanine Campaign **Design Studio** Tom Hingston Studio **Client** Circa Records **Art Directors** Tom Hingston, Robert Del Naja
Designers Tom Hingston, Robert Del Naja **Photographer** Nick Knight

20 **Nomination   Illustration & Photography   Photography National Award**
Silver **Title** One Woman's Wardrobe **Design Studio** Area **Client** Jill Ritblat/Violette Editions **Creative Director** Richard Smith **Designers** Richard Smith, John Dowling
Design Directors Richard Smith, Cara Gallardo **Photographer** Toby McFarlan Pond **Typographers** Richard Smith, John Dowling **Editor** Robert Violette **Publisher** Violette Editions

21 **TV & Cinema Advertising   Public Service/Charity (TV)**
National Award Silver **Title** Torchlight **Agency** Saatchi & Saatchi **Client** COI/Army **Creative Directors** Adam Kean, Alexandra Taylor **Art Director** Alexandra Taylor **Copywriter** Adam Kean
Agency Producer Sally-Ann Dale **Director** Alexandra Taylor **Production Company** Paul Weiland Film Company **Sound Designers** Tot Taylor, Raja Sehgal **Producer** Fran Ratcliffe
Set Designer Andrew Sanders **Client Producer** Barbara Simon **Lighting Camera** Henry Braham **Music Composer/Arranger** Tot Taylor **Editor** John Smith

A town has been attacked by enemy soldiers who have raped a woman; the last thing she wants to see is more soldiers - but not all soldiers are men.

22 **TV & Cinema Advertising   Public Service/Charity (TV)**
National Award Silver **Title** Future Generations **Agency** BBC TV **Client** BBC Brand Marketing **Creative Director** Tim Delaney **Art Director** Ian Ducker **Copywriter** Will Farquhar
Director Chris Palmer **Producer** Sarah Caddy **Production Company** BBC Creative Services **Advertising Agency** Leagas Delaney **Set Designer** Steve Smithwick
Agency Producer Jane Rattle **Editor** Paul Watts **Executive Producer** Steve Kelynack **Special Effects** Shaun Broughton **Music Composer/Arranger** Music Sculptors
Animators Andrew Ruhemann, Paul Berry **Lighting Camera** Howard Atherton

Fond memories of the BBC are recalled with childhood favourites, such as 'Windy Miller' and 'Bagpuss', all narrated by a charming young boy.

but we've tried to give the typeface *Glasgow 1999* some special features.

Glasgow 1999 is a major festival of architecture and design.

24

23 **Promotion**
   National Award Silver **Title** Mother Miniatures **Agency** Mother **Client** Mother **Copywriters** Mark Waites, Ben Mooge **Designers** Richard Walker, Paul Bruce, Libby Brockhoff, Ben Mooge **Design Director** Franklin Tipton **Illustrator** Hugh Beattie **Typographer** Ian Hutchings **Modelmaker** Paul Baker **Producer** Paul Adams

24 **Interactive Media   Distributed Media (CD ROMs, DVDs etc)**
   National Award Silver **Title** Glasgow 1999 Type Movie **Design Studio** MetaDesign **Client** Glasgow 1999 **Creative Design/Director** Tim Fendley **Technical Director** Andreas Harding **Interactive Designers** David Eveleigh, Sam Davy, Frances Jackson **Graphic Designers** David Eveleigh, Sam Davy, Frances Jackson **Programmer** David Eveleigh **Copywriters** Tim Fendley, Sam Davy

MOTHER MINIATURES
ENGLISH FOOTBALL HOOLIGAN SET
1/15 アメリカ現用陸軍歩兵セット
READY TO ASSEMBLE PLASTIC MODEL KIT
MODELLING SKILLS HELPFUL IF UNDER 10 YEARS OF AGE

mm
MOTHER

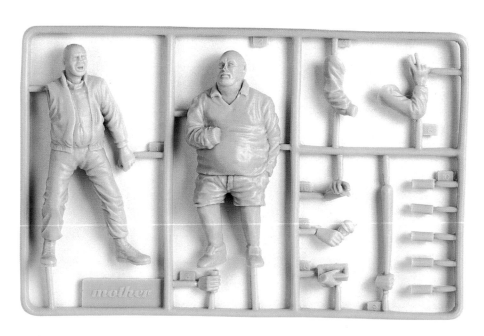

25 **Graphic Design**   Annual Reports, Catalogues, Calendars, Compact Disks & Record Sleeves etc
National Award Silver **Title** Mother Miniatures **Agency** Mother **Client** Mother **Copywriters** Mark Waites, Ben Mooge **Designers** Richard Walker, Paul Bruce, Libby Brockhoff, Ben Mooge
Design Director Franklin Tipton **Illustrator** Hugh Beattie **Typographer** Ian Hutchings **Modelmaker** Paul Baker **Producer** Paul Adams

INDEX

index

SPONSORS

sponsors

SIMPLICITY WILL GET YOU NOTICED

WWW.TONYSTONE.COM

I wonder
what it's like
to catch
a star?

To all of you who reached
for the stars, and especially the few who
actually touched them, congratulations from
all of us who fly close to them every day.
Swisair. We care.

swissair

Ca

► The future of the automobile in 1886: Mercedes-Benz invents the motor car.

ar

Meet Europes best ADs once a week.